CLOSE YOUR CHURCH FOR GOOD
VOLUME 5

CRUCIFORM PASTORAL LEADERSHIP

LEADING THE CHURCH TO FOLLOW JESUS

JEREMY MYERS

CRUCIFORM PASTORAL LEADERSHIP
Leading the Church to Follow Jesus
© 2020 by Jeremy Myers

Published by Redeeming Press
Dallas, OR 97338
RedeemingPress.com

ISBN: 978-1-939992-54-3 (Paperback)
ISBN: 978-1-939992-55-0 (Mobi)
ISBN: 978-1-939992-56-7 (ePub)

Learn more about Jeremy Myers by visiting RedeemingGod.com

Cover Design by Jeremy Myers
Cover Image by Kevin Carden at Lighstock.com

All rights reserved. No part of this publication may be reproduced, stored in or introduced into a retrieval system, or transmitted, in any form, or by any means—electronic, mechanical, photocopying, recording, or otherwise—except for brief quotations, without the prior written permission of both the copyright owner and the publisher of this book.

Unless otherwise stated, all Scripture quotations are taken from the New King James Version˚. Copyright © 1982 by Thomas Nelson, Inc. Used by permission. All rights reserved.

Scripture quotations marked "NIV" are from The Holy Bible, New International Version˚, NIV˚ Copyright © 1973, 1978, 1984, 2011 by Biblica, Inc.˚ Used by permission. All rights reserved worldwide.

JOIN JEREMY MYERS AND LEARN MORE
Take Bible and theology courses by joining Jeremy at
RedeemingGod.com/join/

Receive updates about free books, discounted books,
and new books by joining Jeremy at
RedeemingGod.com/reader-group/

TAKE THE
SKELETON CHURCH
ONLINE COURSE

Join others at
RedeemingGod.com/join/
and take all my courses, including
"The Skeleton Church" online course:

**GET EBOOKS AND THEOLOGY COURSES AT
REDEEMINGGOD.COM/JOIN/**

Thanks for reading!

Books in the *Close Your Church for Good* Series
Preface: Skeleton Church
Vol. 1: The Death and Resurrection of the Church
Vol. 2: Put Service Back into the Church Service
Vol. 3: Church is More than Bodies, Bucks, & Bricks
Vol. 4: Dying to Religion and Empire
Vol. 5: Cruciform Pastoral Leadership

Books in the *Christian Questions* Series
What is Prayer?
What is Faith?
What are the Spiritual Gifts?
What is Hell?
How Can I Study the Bible? (Forthcoming)
Can I Be Forgiven? (Forthcoming)

Other Books by Jeremy Myers
Nothing but the Blood of Jesus
The Atonement of God
The Bible Mirror (Forthcoming)
The Re-Justification of God: A Study of Rom 9:10-24
Adventures in Fishing for Men
Christmas Redemption
Why You Have Not Committed the Unforgivable Sin
The Gospel According to Scripture (Forthcoming)
The Gospel Dictionary (Forthcoming)

Learn about each title at the end of this book

This book is dedicated to all the "Micro-Church" pastors in the world. Don't let anyone look down on you because you are "small."

After all, those who serve in churches of 100 people or less for ten years or more are the ones who keep Christianity alive.

ACKNOWLEDGMENTS

I always thank my wife, Wendy, for every book I write, but I am especially grateful to her for this one. Though no one has ever thought to call her a "Pastor," she is more pastoral than any pastor I have ever known. Myself included. She tirelessly tends, cares, feeds, and protects those whom she loves without ever a thought for praise, titles, recognition, or compensation. If Jesus is the perfect pastoral model, Wendy looks just like Jesus. May my life imitate hers, as she imitates Him.

I also want to thank my father, Bill Myers, for his lifelong service as a pastor. He is one of the pastoral heroes I had in mind when I dedicated this book. Thanks also must be extended to my pastoral mentor, Jim Davey, who encouraged me when I embarked on my first pastoral adventures at the ripe old age of 25. And I will never forget Stephen Hammond, pastor of Mosaic Arlington, who was Jesus for me at a time I needed Him most.

And of course, thank YOU. Thank you for reading this book. You are an encouragement to me, as I hope I am to you.

TABLE OF CONTENTS

INTRODUCTION	13
PART I: RESIGN AS PASTOR	17
PASTORAL PAY	27
Passages on Pastoral Pay	28
Dangers of Paying a Pastor	40
Conclusion	42
Discussion Questions	43
Pastoral Power	47
Passages on Pastoral Power	50
Conclusion	56
Discussion Questions	57
Pastoral Popularity	59
Passages on Pastoral Popularity	61
Conclusion	64
Discussion Questions	65

Saving the Pastor 67
Benefits of Resigning as Pastor 70
How to Make Money After Resigning 76
Get Saved as a Pastor 80
Discussion Questions 81

Part II: Concluding the Sermon 83
Stop Preaching 87
Preaching Texts 88
Cancel the Sermon 99
Healthy Teaching 102
Conclusion 111
Discussion Questions 112

Living the Scriptures 115
Biblical Apprenticeship 116
The Lack of Practice 118
Raising Biblical Literacy 120
Interactive Teaching 123
Interactive Obeying 127
Discussion Questions 131

Part III: Discard the Doctrinal Statement 133
Bad and Ugly Doctrinal Statements 141
Judging Jesus 146

    Creeds Kill 150

    Gutting the Gospel 159

    Discussion Questions 163

Good Doctrine 167

    Three Benefits to Doctrinal Statements 167

    A More Excellent Way 170

    What is the Truth? 173

    Discussion Questions 175

Part IV: Let Prayer Meetings Cease 177

Problem Prayers 181

    Five "Bad Habit" Prayers 181

    Pitfalls of Prayer Meetings 186

    Discussion Questions 188

How Should we Pray? 191

    Passages on Prayer 192

    Pray Without Ceasing 199

    Pray According to the Will of God 202

    Guaranteed Answers to Prayer 206

    Rethinking Prayer Meetings 212

    Discussion Questions 215

Cruciform Pastoral Leadership 219

    Cruciform 219

Pastoral Leadership 221
Cruciform Pastoral Leadership 226
Discussion Questions 227

Appendix I: Preaching, Teaching, and Evangelism 229

Appendix II: 14 Reasons Biblical Illiteracy is Not Bad 239

Join Jeremy Myers and Learn More 295

INTRODUCTION

I love pastors. In general, pastors want to serve, teach, help, and encourage others. They love God, love His Word, and love His people.

Yet pastors have a problem. It is not *their* problem, but a problem put on them by the way we *do* church today. The problem with pastoral ministry is that the way the church is structured today, most pastors cannot actually be the pastors they dream of being. Most pastors feel stuck. Pastors want to shepherd their people, but often end up feeling more like a policeman or fireman, stopping biblical morality crimes and putting out doctrinal or interpersonal fires. Nearly every pastor, no matter how successful, how large their church, or how many books they have in print, feels like they are never quite doing enough, like they never quite measure up.

Some days they blame the people in their congregation. They're not dedicated enough. They don't listen. If only they were more spiritual and spent more time in Scripture, more time in prayer, and more time at church.

But in the quiet hours of the early mornings and sometimes as they stand in the church foyer after preaching an earth-shattering sermon only to hear people mumble "Good sermon, pastor" on their way out the door, they wonder if the problem is with them. They fear that maybe they themselves need to study more, pray more, and serve more. Maybe they need to go back for more education. Maybe they need to try harder, work longer, and preach louder. Maybe they need to switch churches and try a new location. Maybe, however, they're not supposed to be a pastor at all.

But what else could they do? Pastoral ministry is what they're called to. Pastoral ministry is all they've done for 23 years. Pastoral ministry pays the bills. The kids are in college. The marriage is finally getting a bit better. All of this would go away if they resigned as pastor. And what would they do for a living? How would they survive?

These are the sorts of things many pastors are feeling. If you are a pastor, these might be some of the things you are feeling. How do I know?

I know because I was a pastor.

Let me rephrase that.

I know because I *am* a pastor.

I have all those thoughts and feeling described above. Every time the word "they" is used above, substitute in the word "I" and you have an insight into some of the things I have thought during the entire time I have been in pastoral ministry.

And while I am still a pastor, I am no longer a *paid* pastor. I am not on the staff of any "church," but I am still a pastor. Indeed, the pastoral ministry I am currently involved with is more pastoral than ever before. Now that I have left professional pastoral ministry, I have found the freedom and space to be more of a pastor than when I had a "Pastor" sign on my office door. Now that I am not called a pastor or getting paid to pastor, I feel like I am finally pastoring people. I now feel like I am actually helping people. I feel like my relationships with others are genuine. I sense the leading and voice of God in ways that I had only preached about before. I gain new insights and understandings into Scripture like never before, and I never feel like I have to leverage these ideas into sermons that will keep people in the pews and pennies in the offering plate. (It often *feels* like pennies, right?)

I now have the liberty to follow Jesus wherever He leads without any fear or guilt and without any sense of trying to "use" people to support "the Lord's work."

This book tells you how I did it and how you can too!

No, it doesn't.

That's what professional pastors do, and I told you, I'm no longer a professional pastor. I don't have seven steps or three principles or one timeless truth. All I have are some examples of what I did and some ideas for what you can do as well.

This is not a "How To" book. This book is nothing more than a description of the thought process I went through regarding four areas of pastoral ministry. If you are a pastor, you might recognize that some of these thoughts are your own as well. If you are not a pastor, these thoughts might give you some insight on how to help and encourage your pastor. Either way, I hope this book encourages pastors to step out in faith and follow Jesus wherever He leads, even if He leads pastors away from professional pastoral ministry. As we will see, leaving can be a brave form of leading.

PART I:
RESIGN AS PASTOR

One of the most ubiquitous institutional structures which has grown up in the Church through centuries of tradition is the professional clergy, with the resultant clergy-laity dichotomy. ... A professional, distinct priesthood did exist in the Old Testament days. But in the New Testament this priesthood is replaced by two truths: Jesus Christ as our great High Priest, and the Church as a Kingdom of Priests.
—Howard A. Snyder

There is nothing that distorts ministry more than believing you have to make a living by it.
—Wayne Jacobsen

As I sat down to write this book, I just finished reading an online article about megachurch pastor Francis Chan resigning from the church he planted in California. According to the article, he said he wasn't sure why he resigned. All he could say was that he felt a growing conviction that he must resign in order to follow the values and guidelines of the New Testament.

Though other megachurch pastors criticized Chan for resigning when the church was growing so fast and becoming so influential, I believe that such criticism is simply an attempt to quiet similar feelings within their own hearts and minds. I believe God is leading pastors around the country to resign from their jobs and pursue ministry and service as it has been presented in Scripture. The pastors who heed this direction in their hearts know that one of the best ways to lead the church is to lead by example. If a pastor is going to ask the church to follow Jesus in radical and missional ways, to take steps toward loving service of each other and the world, one of the clearest ways a pastor can show he means what he says is by resigning from his paid position as pastor.

So that you know that I myself am leading by example, let me share some of my own story. I want you to know that what I am asking of pastors is not mere theory; I speak from personal experience.

My first pastorate was of a small, struggling church in Northwest Montana. In the church's 25-year history, no pastor had lasted more than three years. But I did. I made it three-and-a-half-years! But half-way through that fourth year of ministry, the church board told me that due to a drop in tithing, they no longer had the funds to pay my salary. They told me I could either resign and find another pastoral position somewhere else, or stay on as pastor and go "bi-vocational."

This was a turning point in my life. I wanted to provide for my wife and our newborn daughter, but I also wanted to be the best pastor I could be, and I wasn't sure I could do all of that while working two part-time jobs. But I loved the church. I loved the people. I loved the area. I wanted to stay on as pastor. I never wanted to be one of those pastors who would say, "In my first church …"

So I had a strong urge to remain the pastor of the church, and find a "secular" job in the community to pay the bills. But I rejected the urge and took another pastorate in another town.

Looking back, I regret that decision. I wish I had stayed. I wish I had pastored without pay.

It had nothing to do with the second church. The second church was more wonderful than the first. The people were more loving, gracious, and kind. I loved the area just as much. But to this day, I feel like I would have learned so much from working in the community, among the people I wanted to love and serve. I would have lost my fear of losing the big tither in church. I would have gained freedom to teach the Scriptures clearly. I would have gained the liberty to lead the people into the community. I don't know what would have happened, but looking back now, it is what I wish I had done.

Leaving that first church set me on the path of "leaving," and after a year and a half in my second pastorate, I resigned so I could return to seminary. Why? Let me bare my heart. I left that second wonderful church because I wanted to get more education so that I could be better qualified to land a pastorate at a larger church, preach on the radio, write books, and join the conference speaking circuit. Sure, I wanted to pastor people and follow the instruction of Jesus to "feed my sheep," but I figured I could do this better if my audience was bigger.

Looking back now, I see that money led me away from my first church, while popularity and power led me away from my second. But I told both churches that I was following God to better fulfil the Great Commission. Isn't it funny how "God" always seems to "lead" church leaders to bigger congregations that offer better pay?

While in seminary, I landed a job at a non-profit organization as a book editor and conference coordinator. As part of my job, I was asked to write various journal articles, and speak at various churches and conferences. After a few years there, I was asked to write a commentary on First Corinthians. I even started a personal newsletter that people subscribed to from all over the country and around the world. I was on my way to achieving all my dreams.

But God had other plans. While I was in seminary, I began to think about some of the issues and ideas I write about in this book. I thought about church and ministry. I thought about pastoral leadership. I thought about following Jesus. Ultimately, I realized that Jesus was not calling me back into pastoral ministry. At least, not into *paid* pastoral ministry. I came to the startling realization that although I was a pastor and will always be a pastor, Jesus didn't want me to get paid for it.

Since I had planned and prepared for pastoral ministry from the age of about five (Yes, I always wanted to be a pastor), the idea that I wouldn't get paid for it was a terrifying thought. How could I support myself? How could I provide for my family? If I wasn't preaching and teaching as a pastor in a church, how could I use the pastoral gifts that I *know* God had given me?

So I decided to go half-way. I decided to go back to what I should have done in that first church. I decided to become "bi-vocational." But since some of my ideas about church and pastoral ministry were non-traditional, I decided that rather than risk splitting or destroying a church, I would plant church. But unlike most church planting efforts of today, I would not seek to raise money or ever ask the church for a paycheck. I wanted to be a "tentmaker" after the example of the Apostle Paul who paid his own way during his ministry by making tents. It seemed to me that God wanted this too, because I had the perfect job for it with this non-profit organization. I could work there, get paid, and plant a church on the side.

That's when the bottom fell out of my life. Partly because of seminary, partly because of my blog, and partly because of my personality, I was "let go" from my job. I hadn't done anything morally wrong, but the CEO of the organization thought it would be better if I didn't work there anymore. I was studying and writing about some ideas that he considered dangerous. None of these areas of study contradicted anything in the organization's doctrinal statement, but he was afraid that my research interests might hinder future donations to the ministry. He asked me to resign. I refused, so he fired me.

Now I was without the "tentmaking" part of tentmaking ministry. I still wanted to plant a church without raising support, but I now had no income. Yet I stuck with my convictions, and rather than go back into paid pastoral ministry, I started looking for a new way to earn a living. I applied for numerous positions in various work fields. But without any experience or education in business or management, no one was willing to hire me. After submitting several hundred résumés, and only getting one interview, I finally landed a job as a carpet cleaner.

It was a good experience for me, but one of the hardest jobs of my life. I worked about eighty hours per week, and got paid $10 per hour. The job was physically exhausting. I was injured on numerous occasions, damaged the tendons of my right hand, and ultimately developed a hernia. I finally had to quit. My body couldn't take it any longer.

I almost went back into the pastorate, because it seemed to be the only thing I was qualified for which would provide an income. But through a long series of events, I ended up becoming a chaplain in a prison. It is a job that was still within my "field" but which is not officially "pastoral ministry" in a church.

Once I got the job, I set about once again trying to plant a church on the side. But during the multi-year process of trying to find work, God had been showing me something deeper about the church He is building in the world. I began to see that the church is not a place or an event. The church is the people of God who follow Jesus into the world. As such, it is technically impossible to "plant a church." The church is already planted, and we just have to figure out how to be involved in the church that already exists.

This growing conviction was infinitely reinforced through my work as a prison chaplain. As a chaplain, I worked closely with people from over twenty different religious groups. I began to see that when it comes to the values and goals of Christianity, we are not much different from most other religions in the world. We all struggle for money, popularity, and power. We all pray and worship in relatively similar ways, with all of us believing that *our* God hears and answers *our* prayers, while pretty much ignoring everybody else. As a first-hand witness to the working of all the major world religions, I began to see that the way the popularized version of the Christian church operates is not that much different from any other world religion.

But I knew that Christianity *was* different. I knew that Jesus was unique and that grace was unheard of among other religions. But if these things were so, how come the way Christianity was practiced and taught was so similar to the way every other world religion was also taught and practiced? As I listened to and compared the various world religions, including Christianity, I realized with a shock that if you changed the names we use and the hats we wear, you could not tell the difference between most of the world religions.

I began to wonder: Is this really what Jesus had in mind? Is this really what the church is supposed to be and do?

I could not believe so. I could not believe that Jesus came just to start another religion that looks and acts and functions like pretty much every other religion. It seemed that so much of the church leadership was focused on little more than cash, credit, and control, or to use other words, many in the church seemed to strive after money, ministry reputation, and manipulation of others. I came to believe that there must be a way for followers of Jesus to be the church in our neighborhoods which does not rely on the worldly values of possessions, popularity, and power.

As my family and I began to explore various avenues on how to live as the church within a community of other people without focusing on how to get cash from them, gain credit for our ministry among them, or control them to do what I wanted, I also began to write books as a way of chronicling the ideas and values about church that we discovered. I am still on this path today. Jesus continues to lead my family and me in new and fresh directions as we learn to be the church in ways I never before imagined.

Due to these exciting new directions Jesus has taken us, we have come to understand that while some people think we have "left" the church, the truth is that we are now more active in the church than ever before. For example, though no one now calls me "Pastor," I believe I have a greater pastoral heart and sensitivity than ever before. My wife and I see daily examples of how God leads us to tend and care for His sheep in ways that we would have ignored and overlooked previously. In other words, though I am not getting paid as a pastor in a church, I am more of a pastor now than ever before.

So while I still regret leaving that first church, I sometimes wonder if I ever would have learned what I know now had I stayed.

Early in my journey toward seeing church as the people of God who follow Jesus into the world, I came to the realization that since pastors are to shepherd the flock of God, this means that pastors are the ones who must lead the church to follow Jesus into the world. It seems obvious to say it, but pastoral leadership begins with the pastor. *If the church is to follow Jesus into the world, the pastor should be the first to go.*

The "Jeremy Myers" of twenty years ago would not have agreed. He would have said that pastoral leadership is best accomplished through preaching, prayer, vision casting, and teaching sound theology. His approach to ministry was "I teach; they go." That "Jeremy Myers" would not have gotten along with the "Jeremy Myers" of today. I would have judged myself, condemned myself, and criticized myself for shirking my pastoral duties. But ironically, the "Jeremy Myers" of today sees himself as more pastoral than at any time he had the word "Pastor" on his door.

Do not misunderstand. I still engage in numerous "pastoral" activities. Though no one calls me "Pastor," I am still pastoral (maybe more than ever before). I write, teach, and preach. I sit with people on a regular basis and talk with them, counsel them, and encourage them in their walk with Jesus. I believe God has given me some good insights into Scripture, theology, mission, and the church, and I want everybody to know what I have learned. I struggle, as do all pastors, with the balance between using my God-given talents to the best of my ability for His kingdom, and using my talents to further my own agenda and make my own name great. However, one of the key factors in finding this balance is my refusal to return to full-time, paid, pastoral ministry.

If you are a pastor, and are considering following some of the other suggestions and ideas in this book, you will need to begin by thinking through some of the suggestions and ideas in the following chapters. You can never lead your church into freedom from the pull of money, popularity, and power, until you lead the way yourself.

But be warned. You may just end up losing your job in the process. Your story may end up looking somewhat like mine. Of course, we serve a creative God, so it is just as possible that your story will look entirely different. Either way, you need to recognize that God may be leading you to resign from paid pastoral ministry so that you can more fully engage in *true* pastoral ministry. The following chapters explain why and how you can do this.

The main point to remember is that the values you may have adopted which currently guide your church and your ministry may not actually be the values of Jesus. The values which guide many pastors and churches are related to how much cash is in the plate, who gets the credit for what is done, and who gets to control what people think, say, and do. Jesus rejected all these things during the wilderness temptations, and to follow in the footsteps of Jesus, we must reject them again today. Though few of us want to admit that we are chasing more pay, power, and popularity, in our more honest moments, we see the pull of these things in much of what we say and do.

The following chapters will consider each of these three pastoral pitfalls along with a look at some of the passages used to defend their practice in the church today. We begin with the pitfall of pastoral pay.

CHAPTER 1

PASTORAL PAY

If you look at the average church budget, the two largest budget items are generally the building and the staff salaries. Which one is in first position depends on the size of the buildings, the newness of the buildings, and how many people are on staff. Quite often, bigger buildings go hand-in-hand with better pastoral salaries, because it is the prominent and popular pastors who can bring in more money to support the costs of "doing church."

As a result, pastors are often equated with the money that a church brings in. The right pastor can bring in a lot of money for the church. But if you have the wrong pastor, all the big tithers might take their money elsewhere. Similarly, whenever there is a budget crisis, usually the first thing that gets cut from the budget is mission-related items. The last thing that usually gets cut is the pastoral salary. When this budget shortfall is ongoing, the church leadership usually responds by asking the pastor to preach a sermon series on tithing. Over the centuries, this practice has created a caricature in the minds of many about the pastoral role. When people think of pastors, they often think of someone who pleads for money. The constant mass mailings from church organizations and the incessant begging for money by televangelists has not helped.

All of this has led many pastors to begin focusing on money themselves. Whether they like it or not, pastors often see their salary and the church budget as indicators of how well they are doing as a pastor. Few pastors would say that they are in ministry for the money, and truthfully, most pastors don't get paid all that well anyway, but nevertheless, our sense of success or failure is often determined by how much money is in the church budget and how much of that budget is allocated for our salary.

To ward against this, a pastor should always be asking himself, "If I wasn't getting paid to do this, would I still do it?" Søren Kierkegaard proposes the following experiment:

> Let us make the thought-experiment—if somebody were able to prove conclusively that Christ never existed at all, nor the Apostles either, that the whole thing was a fabrication—I should like to see how many priests would lay down their office.[1]

Kierkegaard is implying that very few would lay down their office. Why not? Because of the pay. The sad fact is that while many pastors are not in pastoral ministry for the money, they would not be in pastoral ministry at all if it were not for the money. We think that getting paid is being practical, and that a worker is worthy of his wages, but the secret truth is that if it weren't for the money, few pastors would actually remain in their positions.

PASSAGES ON PASTORAL PAY

But does not Scripture provide instruction for churches to pay

---

[1] Søren Kierkegaard, *Attack Upon Christendom* (Boston: Beacon, 1957), 200.

their pastors? While there are several passages that seem to indicate that pastors should get paid, upon closer inspection we see that they do not actually defend the practice of the pastoral salary.

The Levitical Priesthood

Some point to the Levitical Priesthood as proof that spiritual leaders should have their needs met by the people they serve. Passages such as Numbers 18 and Deuteronomy 18 are often referenced in support of this idea. Yet while it is true that Priests serving in the Tabernacle, and later the Temple, could eat of the grain and meat that was brought as sacrifices, it must be noted that this was only for the Priests who were serving *at the time the sacrifice was made*. How often were Priests serving in such capacity? According to 1 Chronicles 23–24, the Priests were divided into 24 divisions, with each division serving about two weeks out of each year. For the rest of the year, they had to provide for their own needs. They did not receive an annual salary. Instead, they had to provide for themselves and their family through other means.

How? While the Levites were not given an inheritance of land in the same way the other Tribes of Israel were, they did receive portions of land around various cities scattered throughout Israel. Numbers 35 indicates that they were allotted 48 cities throughout Israel, and the land around each city extending out from the city walls for 1000 cubits radially in all directions, or 2000 cubits on a side, which is about 900 meters or a little over half a mile (cf. also Joshua 20–21). They were to use this land for their herds and crops.

If the Levitical priests were only serving in the Tabernacle (or Temple) two weeks out of the year, and the rest of the year they dwelled in one of the 48 cities scattered around Israel, what did they do in those cities? They did the same thing every other person did: They lived, worked, and raised their families. They planted crops, raised animals, and worked in their community. *One thing they did not do was live off the tithes of other people.* Remember, the tithes were only brought to Jerusalem during the times of sacrifices and feasts.

So the Levites worked in their cities and the surrounding fields. Some were farmers, while others were herdsman. A few were potters, or weavers. Every trade that could be found in any other city would also be found in a Levitical city. These were not cities filled with a bunch of Bible teachers who sat around reading the Bible and waiting for people to bring them food and meat. No, they worked and earned their living like any other person in the country. The only exception to this was when they had to leave their home for two weeks out of every year to serve in Jerusalem. At those times, they ate from the sacrifices and offerings which people brought. And it appears that they brought sacrifices and offerings as well from their own crops and herds. They were part of the *giving* group rather than the sole receivers of what others gave.

In the days of Jesus, things had changed a bit, and many of the priests permanently lived and worked in the Temple. Furthermore, they had acquired numerous fields around Jerusalem upon which to grow their Temple wheat and barley. Also, through money-changing and the sale of sacrificial animals which were without blemish (see John 2:12-22), many of the Temple Priests had become quite wealthy.

Yet the presence of such practices did not indicate divine approval for them. On the contrary, Jesus often criticized the religious leaders for these very things (cf. Matt 23:23-24; Luke 20:46-47). The religious leaders in the days of Jesus were leveraging the Mosaic Law to make themselves rich while neglecting the poor and needy in their midst. When the people brought their tithes and offerings in obedience to the instructions of the religious leaders, all that the leaders offered in return were empty prayers and promises of divine blessing. This was exactly the opposite of what God intended, but seems to be hauntingly familiar to much of what goes on in many churches today. How many pastors have been enriched and how many glorious buildings have been constructed on the backs of the poor and needy in our communities?

All of this indicates that it is nearly impossible to obtain a defense for pastoral salaries from the practices of the Levitical Priesthood. The nail in the coffin to this idea, however, is found in the Priesthood instituted by Jesus through His death and resurrection. According to 1 Peter 2:5-9, all believers are now priests. We are a kingdom of priests, with Jesus as the only High Priest (cf. Hebrews 8). When all of us are "priests," we cannot make false division between a priestly class and a non-priestly class. Therefore, there is no priestly class which can depend on the non-priestly class to provide for their daily needs. The church, therefore, cannot look to the Levitical Priesthood to support of the practice of pastoral salaries.

Acts 20:33-35

How often have you heard a sermon about tithing based on Acts 20:35: "It is more blessed to give than to receive"? Yet the context reveals that this passage is not about people tithing to the church or to pastoral ministry at all. Instead, it is teaching exactly the opposite.

In Acts 20, Paul is providing instructions to a group of elders from Ephesus. In verses 33-34, Paul reminds them that he has not been paid with gold and silver, or even with clothing, but has provided for his own needs, as well as those who travelled with him. He did this so that he and his companions would not have to accept payment from anybody in Ephesus. From statements Paul makes elsewhere, this seems to be his normal approach to ministry. He made tents for a living to provide for his needs while he traveled and taught in the churches (cf. Acts 18:1-3; Php 4:14-16). And according to verse 34, Paul not only provided for his own needs through tentmaking, but also for the needs of those who travelled with him! Though we often hear of "Tentmaking pastors," I have yet to hear of one who not only provides for himself but also for the other members on his ministry team! Yet this is what Paul did.

After this description of his own ministry, Paul instructs the Ephesian elders to follow his example. He tells them that they also should labor with their hands as he has, so that they can support the weak (Acts 20:35). While some believe that the weak are those who do not understand why an elder should get paid to teach the Scriptures, it is more likely that the weak are those who are unable to provide for themselves. By working with their hands, the elders not only provide for their own needs without depending on the financial support of others, but also help provide for the physical needs of those who are unable to work. These would include people like orphans, widows, and the sick, or even ministry partners who are not able to work.

The closing statement of Paul is a quotation from Jesus: "It is more blessed to give than to receive." This does not mean, as some pastors preach, that the people in the pews are more blessed when they give to the church than when they receive from the church. Quite to the contrary, Paul is telling the spiritual leaders of the Ephesian church that it is more blessed for *them* to give to the needy in the church than it is for them to receive money and support from those among whom they minister.

A proper understanding of Acts 20:33-35 reveals that pastors cannot use this verse to encourage greater generosity in tithing. Instead, if this passage says anything about the relationship between a pastor and money, it is that the pastor should give sacrificially from his own income to help the poor and needy in the church, and also financially support (if he is able) those who partner with him in the ministry.

So ironically, the very passage that pastors use to encourage people to give, is actually saying that pastors should be the ones to give. When pastors preach "It is more blessed to give than to receive" the people in the pews have every right to stand up and shout, "You first!" for that is the instruction Paul is providing in Acts 20:35.

1 Corinthians 9:1-18

At first, this text seems to conflict with what Paul told the Ephesian elders in Acts 20. First Corinthians 9 contains Paul's defense of his right as an apostle to receive money from the people he ministers among. Paul goes on to argue that although he has the right to receive money, he refused to exercise that right.

Paul compares the apostolic ministry to soldiers who go to war and workers who tend fields. They enjoy the fruits of their labors, argues Paul, and so also should an apostle. He supports his case with a quotation from Deuteronomy 25:4 about not muzzling an ox while it treads out the grain (9:9-10), and also mentions the biblical precedent of the priests serving in the temple who get to partake of the offerings and sacrifices that are brought in (9:13-14). In such ways, Paul clearly defends his right to receive payment for his work as an apostle. He goes on, however, to explain why he has given up this right so as not to be a stumbling block to anyone (9:15-18).

So does this passage mean that pastors of a local church have the right to take a salary? Not quite. Paul is only defending the right of *apostles* to receive income from the people among whom they labor. An apostle is someone who does not stay in one area, but travels from town to town, carrying the message of the gospel with them to new and unreached areas. They plant the seeds of the gospel, and encourage initial spiritual growth among those who believe, and then after a while—anywhere from a few days to a few years—move on to a new location to spread the gospel elsewhere.

That Paul is clearly talking about traveling apostolic teachers is evidenced not only by his frequent references to "apostles" throughout the passage, but also the statements in verses 5 and 7 about taking a believing wife along with them, and soldiers going off to war. With such images, Paul shows he is talking about the teacher who travels away from his home and place of employment to go serve and teach in other cities and towns.

The images of a man who plants a vineyard and the oxen who treads out the grain support this perspective. Most often, we read these verses to say that the vineyard *owner* is the one who plants the vineyard and enjoys its harvest, and the oxen *owner* is the one who should not muzzle the ox, but let it eat some grain at the mill. This, however, does not reflect what actually happened in the culture or what these images mean.

First, a vineyard owner rarely planted and worked his own vineyard. Rather, he would hire people to plant and tend the vines for him. As part of their pay, these hired laborers were allowed to eat of the grapes while they pruned and harvested. Similarly, no oxen owner would ever muzzle his own oxen while it was treading out the grain. This would be like a modern day farmer allowing his tractor to run out of gas. So Deuteronomy 25:4 refers to the scenario of a man who borrows his neighbor's oxen. In such a case, the man should not try to boost his own profits by muzzling his neighbor's oxen so they cannot eat while treading out the grain. This is cruel to the oxen and does not show appreciation to the man who owns the oxen.[2] Again, to use modern farming imagery, this would be like borrowing your neighbor's tractor, using it all day, and then returning it with an empty gas tank. Such things should not happen.

Paul is comparing himself (and all apostles) to borrowed oxen, a traveling soldier, or someone who tends another man's field. To take the gospel to other areas, an apostle must leave their house and job and travel to other areas where they must usually depend on the hospitality and provision of others. Paul, however, as a tentmaker, had a profession which travelled with him, or at least allowed himself to get work with other tentmakers in the various cities he traveled to (cf. Acts 18:1-3). Not all apostles enjoyed such flexibility with their trade, and so they were dependent upon others to provide for their needs while they travelled away from

---

[2] Jan L. Verbruggen, "Of Muzzles and Oxen: Deuteronomy 25:4 and 1 Corinthians 9:9" in *Journal of the Evangelical Theological Society* 49:4 (December 2006): 699-711.

home. Nevertheless, when they returned home, to their families and to their jobs, they no longer depended on others, but labored with their own hands to provide for their own needs. This, as we have seen, was Paul's instructions to the Ephesian elders who stayed in Ephesus, and, we presume, the same instructions he gave to all church elders and leaders everywhere he went.

So 1 Corinthians 9 cannot be used by pastors to defend the practice of receiving a salary. The passage is talking about traveling missionaries and apostolic leaders who have left their home and jobs to teach and support other Christians in other towns. Since they will typically only be in a city or town for a few weeks or months, they are dependent upon the hospitality of the people in that city or town. Ideally, even these spiritual leaders should have "travelling professions" if possible, so that they do not have to depend on the financial aid of others.

Pastors, however, stay in one area, and Paul's instruction to them is that they work hard with their hands, providing for themselves, their families, and the weaker members of the church with the income they receive from their trade.

1 Timothy 5:17-18

First Timothy 5 contains nearly the same arguments as First Corinthians 9. Paul even quotes the same passage out of Deuteronomy 25:4. Here, however, Paul is not talking about apostles who travel to another town to minister, but elders who stay in one place. If there is any text in Scripture which provides guidance on paying pastors and elders in a local church, this is it. Paul says that elders who preach and teach are worthy of a double honor, and that a worker is worthy of his wages.

Though some argue that the concept of "double honor" does

not refer to payment, the context indicates otherwise. First, Paul is indeed talking about wages in the immediate context. Furthermore, in 1 Timothy 5:3, Paul writes that widows deserve to be "honored" which, in that context, means that their daily needs are to be met by the church. This is most easily done with providing widows an income for their needs, though their needs could be met in other ways as well. However, what is curious about this text is that while many pastors use it to defend their own right to receive a salary, I have never heard of a church that honors widows in a similar fashion.

Nevertheless, even though honoring the widows does refer to taking care of their daily and physical needs (possibly through a financial allotment), this does not necessarily mean that a pastor or elder receiving a double honor means that he should receive a financial allotment.

For example, in the context, who is the worker who is worthy of his wages? The way this verse is most often used, one would think that the worker is anyone who works in "full time pastoral ministry." Sadly, no such thing exists in the New Testament. There is no such thing as the clergy-laity division that exists in many groups today. Instead, in the church, every person is a full-time minister (Eph 4:12). God expects every follower of Jesus to have a ministry. To accomplish this ministry, He gives to each person a set of skills, gifts, and abilities. Those who are often called "pastors" generally have skills and abilities in areas of administration, leadership, encouragement, caring, and teaching.

Yet even though everyone is technically in "full-time ministry," why do we pay only one type of minister, the one with the gift of pastor-teacher? Is there any reason other than that these ministers who are getting paid say that they must get paid for what they do? Why is it we pay the "ministers" who have these gifts, but not the "ministers" with other gifts?

First Timothy 5:17-18 does not justify such a distinction, except possibly in one area. In the context of Paul's words, the one who deserves wages is the one who devotes himself to the Word and doctrine. It seems that if we are going to use Scripture to defend our practice of paying pastors, then only pastors who devote time to studying and teaching Scripture and theology should receive any kind of payment.

But what kind of payment, and how much? Well again, some have argued that if "honor" in 1 Timothy 5:3 means paying widows enough to live on, "double honor" in 5:17 means paying pastors twice as much. Yet upon closer inspection, it does not appear that the passage supports this practice of pastoral salaries after all. In this letter, Paul is writing to Timothy, one of the elders in the church of Ephesus. He has already instructed the Ephesian elders to provide for their needs with the work of their own hands (Acts 20:33-35). If they were following his instructions, they would not need the same "honor" that was being given to the widows.

They were, however, allowed to receive the "double honor" which is not an additional salary, but gifts—probably of food or money—from individuals in the congregation who were appreciative for the study and teaching that the elder provided. Today, we might call this an "honorarium." Paul seems to indicate that while giving the double honor is not required, if a particular elder devotes time on his nights and weekends (after he has worked his regular job) to study and prepare quality Bible teaching for those who gather, then if someone wants to give him a gift of appreciation, the elder has the right to accept it.

These gifts of appreciation are not to be expected or demanded (cf. 1 Pet 2:5-9). They are not to evolve into a full-time salary. They are simply gifts given to those who lead the church well, especially in the areas of the word and doctrine. How much should the gifts be? The text does not say. It is up to the individual, and what they want to give to the elder who has helped them understand Scripture in a greater way.

So after looking at the main texts used to defend the practice of pastoral pay, the bottom line conclusion is that there really does not seem to be any Scriptural basis for paying a salary to a pastor.

At the same time, there is no command against it either. What this means is that the question of paying a pastor is up to the individual gatherings of believers, and whether not they think the cost of paying a pastor is worth what they receive in return. According to some recent reports, the average annual pastoral salary is about $84,000. If we simply compare the number of years a typical pastor must attend school for his degrees, this might be too low, especially when doctors and lawyers receive a similar number of years of education and earn much more.

However, when a church decides to pay a pastor, the salary is not the only expense that comes with it. Typically, along with a pastoral salary, a local church must also bear the cost of a church mortgage and all the related expenses of electricity, maintenance, insurance, and numerous other expenses. So in a smaller church, the pastoral salary typically makes up about half of the annual budget.

Therefore, when a church is trying to decide whether or not to pay a pastor, the question is not "Does the Bible tell us to?" (for it doesn't), but rather, "How much will the pastor cost, and could this same amount of money be better spent in other ways to reach our community with the gospel?"

Nevertheless, the lack of Scriptural support for paying a pastor does not mean it is wrong to pay a pastor. All it means is that we do not have explicit Scriptural instructions for the practice. I can think of numerous situations where paying a pastor to perform certain tasks for a group of believers might be a wise course of action. However, no church should pay someone to be a pastor simply because "other churches do it." If you are going to pay someone, make sure the reasons are crystal clear and the inherent dangers are fully understood … for there are indeed dangers to paying a pastor.

DANGERS OF PAYING A PASTOR

In light of the foregoing study on the key texts about pastoral pay, we have uncovered three dangers that are inherent to paying a pastor.

Spectator Sport

One of the main problems with paying a pastor is that people often begin to develop a spectator mentality. By paying a "professional" they sometimes get the idea that they are paying someone else to "do the work of the ministry" so they can sit back, relax, and enjoy the show. Nobody ever puts it this bluntly, but actual practice shows how widespread this mentality is within churches that have paid pastoral staff. Also, the practice of paying the pastor tends to exalt his spiritual gift above the spiritual gifts of others. Why should the person who has the gift of pastor-teacher get paid for what they do in the church while those with the gift of mercy, evangelism, or service do not? Paying the pastor creates a spiritual gift hierarchy, which damages the Body of Christ. If a church is going to pay a pastor, it might be best to pay him more as a contractor, for a specific purpose, with a specific goal, for a specific time, to fill a specific void in the spiritual-gift mix of the body, or to provide a certain function or perform a certain task, which the church believes is necessary to move the church forward in the directions God has for it. Just don't default to the "we have to have a paid pastor" tradition.

Proper Pay Rate

Second, if a church decides to pay a pastor who devotes time to study and teaching, I do believe that such a pastor could get paid. The Body of Christ needs sound biblical teaching, and (as I have learned myself through my own teaching and writing), it is very difficult to support one's family when one devotes a large amount of time to study, preaching, and teaching.

But if a group of people is going to support a teaching pastor, numerous questions must be asked in order to determine a proper rate of pay. For example, how often does he teach? How long does it take him to prepare? What is his educational background? How many years of experience does he have? What is the comparable pay for people in the church who have similar years of education and experience? How much is his teaching worth to you? These, and other similar questions, might help you determine what your gathering could pay a pastor. Based on this, most pastors should probably be getting paid about double what they are. If you are going to pay your pastor, pay him properly. At the same time, if you pay your pastor, make sure you are getting what you pay for.

Let the Pastor Decide

Third, though I believe that in general, pastors should not receive a full-time salary from the church, no church that has a salaried pastor should ever ask him to stop taking a salary. Unless there are budgetary reasons for asking a pastor to step down, the decision to not take a salary should be fully in the hands of the pastor himself. If and when a pastor personally feels compelled to free himself from the church salary, there are steps he must take to move in that direction. These steps are too painful and too difficult to do overnight, especially when forced upon you from the outside. These transition steps can also take a long time, up to 10 years or more. These steps will be discussed later in this book.

CONCLUSION

So after all is said and done, I am not completely opposed to churches paying a pastor. I simple do not believe the practice can be defended with Scripture. Yet a lack of biblical support doesn't mean the practice is wrong; it just means that before a church decides to pay their pastor, they must carefully consider the pros and cons of the practice. To do this, the church must ask some tough questions.

Questions that must be asked include:

> If we pay a pastor a salary, will the benefits outweigh the costs? Brainstorm about what else could be done in the community or around the world with that same amount of money that would be spent on a salary. Would such ideas be a better use of money than paying a pastor?

> If we pay a pastor to lead the church, will this cause the people in

the church to think that we are paying him/her to do the work of the ministry?

If we pay the pastor, what are we telling the congregation about their ministry in the church, for which they do not get paid?

I would make one other recommendation to help clarify some of these issues in the minds of the congregation. If you are going to pay someone to teach the Bible, organize the church for ministry, provide counseling services, be a CEO of the church, and be a visionary leader for the church, then don't call them "Pastor." Call him a "Permanent Church Consultant," a "Church Manager," a "Spiritual Lifecoach," the "Professional Church Administrator" or something else. Such a move will help remove the false and damaging clergy-laity division that creates so much inertia in the church. It will show that this person is not getting paid because their spiritual gift is better than everybody else's, but instead, this person is getting paid because the church has decided to pay someone who can specifically help the church accomplish its God-given mission in the world.

With all of this in mind, let us move on to the second pitfall in pastoral ministry: pastoral power. This is the subject of the next chapter.

DISCUSSION QUESTIONS

Note: All discussion questions in this book are directed primarily toward pastors and church leaders. As such, personal pronouns such as "you" and "your" will be used. If you are not in a position of church leadership, then when you read these questions, you may substitute

> *in terms such as "my pastor" and "the church leaders" in place of the pronouns.*

1. In your own words, what does *true* pastoral ministry look like? What activities does it involve? Do you get to do these things at least fifty percent of the time in your current ministry?

2. If you could dream up a job description for yourself, what types of activities would it include? How many of these things are you able to do in your current ministry position?

3. Other than your current church ministry position, is there another job you feel you could do that would allow you to earn enough to live on? If so, what is it? If you performed this job, would you also have enough time to minister to others in the ways described in Question 2 above?

4. How much do you get paid in your current ministry position? If the church had that much extra money to serve the community, what sorts of ministries might get accomplished?

5. How often do you give "tithing" sermons and ask people to increase their giving? How does this make you feel?

6. What does the Levitical Priesthood teach about the ancient biblical model for "pastoral" pay?

7. What does Acts 20:33-35 say about the relationship between pastors and money?

8. What does Paul say in Acts 20:33-35 about how pastors should provide for themselves? How does Paul's own life depict this?

9. What can we not use 1 Corinthians 9 to defend the practice of pastoral salaries?

10. What is being referenced in 1 Timothy 5:17-18 when Paul writes about elders receiving "double honor"?

CHAPTER 2

PASTORAL POWER

Power is another great pitfall and temptation for many pastors. It is not that power is evil. Power is good. After all, God has power, Jesus ministered with power, and the Holy Spirit comes in power.

The problem with power is that it can corrupt. It can be used in ways for which it was never intended. Power, when mixed with pride, becomes dangerous, damaging, and destructive. In a pastoral position, the opportunities to misuse and abuse power are all magnified. Power can especially become damaging when those with power seek to control the lives, thoughts, and actions of others.

It is for this reason that if a pastor struggles with power, it might be best for him to resign as pastor. Doing so will not cause the desire for power to simply disappear, but instead, will simply help hinder this pastor from the opportunity to misuse the pastoral position in damaging and abusive ways.

Of course, few pastors actually believe that they struggle with power. So the first thing is to discern whether or not it is *your* struggle. Here are a few diagnostic questions to help make that determination:

- Do you feel like you hold the keys to heaven and hell, determining who is saved, and who is not?

- Do you require Bible study leaders and Sunday school teachers to get approval from you for their curriculum or lesson plans?

- Do you see yourself as the one who decides about doctrinal differences within the church?

- Do you have your seminary degrees hung on your office wall?

- Do you require that people call you "Pastor," "Reverend," or "Doctor"?

- Do you frequently remind people that you are the one with the seminary degree?

- Do you put letters such as M.Div., Th.M., or Ph.D. on your business cards and letterhead?

- Do you feel that people's lives will be better if they just listen to you and do what you say?

- Do you require the music team to get their song selections approved by you?

- Do you require the youth leader to check with you before they do a mission's outreach or community service event?

- Do you "invite" people to leave the church when they disagree with you, your theology, your ideas, or the direction you are leading the church?

- Do you frequently use the phrase "God told me" in your sermons, Bible studies, board meetings, and regular conversations?

Even if you answered "Yes" to one or two of these questions, this does not necessarily indicate that you have a power problem. But if you answered "Yes" to three or more, and then also spend some time in your head justifying why you behave in this way, it is likely that you struggle with the lure of pastoral power, and should consider resigning as pastor so that you do not harm the people under your care.

In fact, how does the simple suggestion that you resign from your pastoral position make you feel? If you got defensive and angry, this also is a likely indicator that you struggle with the lure of pastoral power.

I know how you feel. I felt the same way before I resigned from pastoral ministry. I struggled with pastoral power, and could have answered "Yes" to over half of the questions on that list above. But I justified my behavior because I knew that "God had called me to the ministry." I knew that "I had the gift of pastor-teacher." I knew that if people just listened to me and what I preached, their lives would be so much better. I was doing so much good for them. They needed me.

So I understand the fear and the frustration. I was once there myself. But I have learned that the lust for power diminishes after you have resigned as pastor. Very few of the temptations described above are possible for those who are not paid, professional, full-time pastors. Furthermore, even if God did call you to the pastorate and you truly are helping people, one of the best ways to help lead the people of your church toward freedom in Christ and life in the Spirit may be to resign as pastor so that they stop following you and start following Jesus Christ as the sole Head of the Church. In such a way, you are not leading as the head, nor leading from a position of power and authority, but are choosing instead to walk the path of discipleship with them, joining in their struggles and fears, learning from each other as you participate in life together. This is true pastoral ministry.

Nevertheless, there are several passages from the Bible that we pastors like to use to justify our role as God's spokesman and mouthpiece on earth. These passages convince us that our use of power is God's will for the people He has placed under our care. But as we will see, such an understanding of these passages is contrary to the revelation of God in Scripture as well as the example of Jesus Christ.

PASSAGES ON PASTORAL POWER

Just as history is written by the victors, it is also true that the rules are created by those in power. Pastors are no exception. We are experts in using Scripture and theology to reinforce our power. We use our knowledge of Greek and Hebrew, our sense of spiritual calling, our ordination, the seminary degrees, leadership skills, and charismatic personalities to convince people that they must follow and obey. Then we preach, teach, and write about how we are the authorities on spiritual matters, and the people "under our care" must listen to us, follow us, and obey us.

If you have been around church for any length of time, you know how damaging and destructive this can be, not only on the congregations, but also in the pastor's life and family.

One way to begin freeing ourselves from the bondage of power that we put on others and upon ourselves is to unravel the biblical texts that have been used to support our claim to power and authority. There are dozens of such passages, but some of the more prominent are discussed below.

I Give You Power and Authority

Passages in which Jesus gives authority to His disciples are popular texts for the idea that pastors have a special type of God-ordained power (e.g., Matt 28:18, Luke 10:19). Sometimes it is pointed out that "pastor" is one of the foundational spiritual gifts given to the church (Eph 4:11-15). Occasionally, the promise of power through the Holy Spirit is also used (Acts 1:8). Frequently, pastors will talk about their divine calling (Acts 16:9), their special knowledge (1 Cor 12:8), their visionary leadership (Prov 29:18), and numerous other verses to back up such ideas.

The truth about all such passages is that the power and authority which Jesus gave is not just given to a select few individuals, but is given to all followers. The power and authority is given to the church, not just to a person or specific group of people within the church. And while it is true that the gift of pastor (or pastor-teacher) is a foundational gift, this does not make it a better gift than any of the others.[1] The Holy Spirit is within all be-

---

[1] See Jeremy Myers, *God's Blueprints for Church Growth* (Dallas, OR: Redeeming Press, 2020) for more on this concept.

lievers, giving everyone gifts, all of which are necessary and important. And while it may be true that pastors are called by God to minister, every believer is also likewise called by God to minister with their spiritual gifts as well. Divine calling is not unique to pastors.

The bottom-line truth regarding power and authority is that the power and authority which God has given to the church is just that—it is given *to the church*. It is not given to the pastor alone. The pastor is not the focal point of God's power and authority in the church. Any time a pastor starts to bring up some of the ideas and verses mentioned above as proof about his authority and power in the church and why others should listen to him and obey, red flags should go up and alarm bells should sound. Such pastors are only trying to usurp the power of God in the church for themselves. The power which God has given to the church is a power shared and practiced by all.

Spiritual Fathers

Another area where some pastors try to exert power is in the area of "spiritual fatherhood." This concept is not found in all churches, but in those churches that do practice "spiritual fatherhood," the pastor often uses this idea to exert his authority and control the lives of others.

The idea of spiritual fathers comes from passages like 1 Corinthians 4:15-16, 11:1, Philippians 2:22, 4:9, 1 Thessalonians 2:11, 2 Timothy 3:10, 14, and 1 John 2:13-14. Such passages are used by some pastors to imply that they have the right to rule and guide the people in their church.

To properly understand these passages, let us consider the example of Paul. Paul tells those under his care to follow his instructions and imitate his example because they are his children in the gospel. From this, certain pastors also try to get the people of their church to follow their instructions, and imitate their example.

The primary problem with this line of reasoning, however, is that not all pastors are like the Apostle Paul. The ministry of Paul was characterized by self-sacrificial service to others. Many pastors who try to control the thinking and behavior of others with the concept of "spiritual fatherhood" are more concerned with their own position of power and prominence than they are with the spiritual well-being of other people. This can be seen when their practice of spiritual fatherhood goes far beyond anything Paul practiced in his life and ministry. If Paul was a "spiritual father" he was a father who served others, not a father who lorded his position over others. Paul, as a spiritual father, did not engage in spiritual child abuse.

Paul gave up food and money to minister to others, but many "spiritual fathers" today command their people to tithe 10%, and some even go to the extent of demanding that people submit monthly financial records to show where their money is going. Furthermore, while Paul allowed others to make their own choices, some "spiritual fathers" today want families to check with him regarding such things as vacation planning, job transfers, financial management, and child rearing. None of the instructions Paul gives in the passages above fall into such areas.

Beyond this, it appears that Paul's situation was much different than the pastoral "spiritual fathers" of today. Aside from being an apostle, the people who followed Paul as their spiritual father appear to have done so by their own choice. Paul did not believe that just because someone placed faith in Jesus for eternal life as a result of his ministry, that this meant he could direct their lives and force them to do whatever he wanted. He never demanded any sort of submission to him or his ministry, nor did he dictate the actions or behaviors of others, but instead, he always invited people to make their own choices. Certainly, he presented his own life as an example and believed that he was following the example of Jesus, but this is very different than demanding that people obey and listen to him alone. Quite to the contrary, this controlling and manipulative sort of behavior is exactly what some of the false teachers were doing, and Paul criticized them for it.

It should also be noted that Jesus instructed His followers to not call anyone father, since we have only one Father, God in heaven (Matt 23:8-11). This instruction is not just about the title "father" (or Pastor or Reverend), but as with all the instructions from Jesus, is about the attitude of the heart. One who is a pastor and shepherd of the church of God does not show his care and concern for others by demanding that they obey and follow him in all ways. Such behavior does not reveal the proper condition of the heart for one who is a pastor in the church, but in fact reveals the exact opposite.

So be wary. Be on guard against any desire to rule, control, or manipulate the actions and behavior of others. If you believe something strongly, yes, fulfil your responsibility to teach what you believe and present the arguments for it. This is, after all, what I am doing in this book. But never believe that you have the right to tell others what they *must* do if they are true followers of Jesus.

Similarly, be on your guard against any pastor who demands that you think of him as your spiritual father. For our true Spiritual Father, God in heaven, waits patiently for us to see His love and care, so that we freely make the choice to follow Him. If a pastor is really going to lead, teach, and encourage you, this will come through your own choice, not through his demands that you do so. Any human who follows the example of God wins over others, not by force or exerting control, but through loving service and self-sacrifice for the sake of others. Any other form of pastoral power is not following the example of Jesus.

The Head of the Church

Sometimes, those of us who are pastors think of ourselves as the head of the local church, the spiritual leader that deserves respect and obedience from others, or the one like a High Priest who has the closest connection to God.

Among the disciples of Jesus and in the early church there were spiritual leaders who thought of themselves in such a manner. Some of the early believers wanted to sit in places of honor and privilege (cf. Matt 20:21-24; Jas 2:1-13), and receive recognition for their leadership role within the church. This seems to have been a problem in Corinth also, as Paul reminded the believers in Corinth that the church has only one head, Jesus Christ.

Many of the early Christians came out of Judaism and pagan religions where a class of clerics and priests ruled and dominated other people in all spiritual matters. So also, the concept of a man as the head of the household carried over into the idea that the pastor was the head of the church. This practice was reinforced in early churches since these groups often met in houses.

Scripture argues against a single, authoritarian leader in a church, and teaches instead that all are equal in Jesus, that spiritual gifts were given to all for the benefit of all, and that all are priests of God with Jesus as the High Priest (cf. Matt 26:6-11; 1 Pet 2:5, 9; Heb 4–5).

Ultimately, the cure for the temptation to be the single authoritarian head is to see Jesus as the sole head of the church. There are no sub-heads in the church, nor are Jesus and pastors conjoined twins. We do not share headship over one body. Jesus is the head, and the pastor is part of that body. When we view ourselves this way, we begin to see that our role in the church is the same as everybody else's. We are all members of the family of God and are given gifts so that we all might serve one another.

CONCLUSION

Pastoral power is another key consideration in redeeming the pastoral position. Some pastors thrive off the power that comes with their position. They like being the man in charge, the one who holds the keys to heaven and hell, the local theology and Bible expert, and the one who can sway masses with a turn of his golden tongue. Some take pride in being called "Pastor" or "Reverend" and require such titles from their people. Others enjoy the seat of honor at every table, seeing their picture on the foyer wall, and having the reserved parking spot closest to the front door.

Leaving the professional pastorate will not necessarily remove the desire for power and prominence. There are, after all, numerous people in *unpaid* leadership positions within the church who also have a lust for power and prominence. This is true in traditional churches that have lots of paid staff, and house churches that have no staff. Pride and lust for power are vast problems and we must all do what we can to protect ourselves from them.

So we have looked at two pastoral pitfalls, that of pastoral pay and pastoral power. The final pitfall to protect ourselves against is that of pastoral popularity. This is the topic of the next chapter.

DISCUSSION QUESTIONS

1. This chapter began with several questions for you to ask yourself. Go back and look through them again. Did you answer "Yes" to any of these questions? If so, why do you think each of these are important to you?

2. To whom did God really give power and authority? Was it just to the apostles? Was it just to pastors and ministry leaders? Or was it to the church as a whole?

3. What actions did Paul engage in as a "spiritual father"? Did he consolidate his power and silence all who questioned him and his authority? Or did he use his position to sacrificially love and serve others? Give some examples to support your answer.

4. If Jesus is the sole Head of the church, what role does the pastor play in the "Body of Christ"?

What fears do you have if you were to give up your position as a leader in the church? Are these fears based on actual evidence? Do these "fears" still materialize in churches that have professional pastors and leaders? (For example, many claim that without regular preaching and teaching from a professionally-trained pastor, the people will fall into heresy. But many churches struggle with false teaching *because* of the pastor.)

CHAPTER 3

PASTORAL POPULARITY

Pastoral popularity is a common area of downfall for many pastors. It often seems that churches are in an "American Idol" competition for who has the best pastor. Ideally, churches often look for the pastor who is the best-looking, best-dressed, and best-educated. They want someone who is a great speaker, is outgoing, friendly, and good with people. If possible, it would also be good for the pastor to be a well-known author, conference speaker, and radio or TV teacher.

Churches that get all this in a pastor often become known in the community, not by their love for one another, how they serve others, or how well they reflect Jesus Christ, but by the name of the pastor. For example, when I lived in Dallas, there were several famous churches in town, and though I often heard people speak about the church, I cannot remember anyone ever referring to the church by its name. Instead, people spoke of "Chuck Swindoll's church" or "the church of T. D. Jakes."

If you live in a city that has a Christian Superstar, and you have friends or family visit from out of town, what church is it they want to visit on Sunday? If you asked them, it probably wouldn't be your church. Instead, they probably want to go see the great pastor, the world-renowned author, the television evangelist, the Christian Superstar. They want to see the show.

It is for these reasons that when I lived in Dallas, I never once went to any of the churches with big-name popular pastors. I even stayed away from most of the mega-churches. While I like the teaching of Chuck Swindoll and Tony Evans, I never visited their churches a single time. I never visited First Baptist Dallas or Fellowship Church. Even though I think these churches are doing some good things, I decided to boycott the whole business. I did not want to get swept up into the cult of the personality.

Yet this cult of the personality is what many pastors strive for and thrive upon. They want to be well-known. They want to have hundreds of thousands of followers on Twitter. They desire the radio spot and the television primetime interview. While I am all in favor of spreading the message of the gospel using all available methods of modern technology, I am just not sure that the requirements of such methods mesh well with the requirements for pastoral ministry.

It seems that when one looks at the biblical model for a spiritual leader, the character traits that rise to the top are not good hair, self-advancement, and a career mindset, but humility, service, and compassion. Again, I understand that most pastors are quite humble, service-oriented, and compassionate leaders. But I also know from experience that being a full-time, paid pastor comes with certain expectations about what you will look like, and how your career will advance. Your church must get bigger. You should develop an online following through a blog and website. If you could get a book published, it would be great, but two would be better, and one of them should be a best-seller. Your sermons must be good enough to get broadcast on the radio, or at the bare minimum, through a podcast on the internet. If these things aren't happening, people begin to wonder if you are a good pastor.

Though resigning as pastor will not automatically remove all these goals and desires, it does help divorce these dreams from the pastoral position. There is nothing wrong with getting a website, publishing books, starting a podcast, or teaching on the radio, unless you think that these things will prove you are a good pastor. By resigning as pastor, the temptation to leverage your position to increase your popularity and fame disappears, because the position is not there to leverage.

Let us look at a couple passages which have been used to defend the idea that God blesses good pastors with popular ministries. In so doing, we will see that numbers mean nothing when it comes to God's pleasure over a particular pastoral ministry.

PASSAGES ON PASTORAL POPULARITY

Numerous Scriptural passages are used to defend the practice of gaining popularity and gathering large followings. Let us consider a few of the more "popular" texts.

The Gospels

There are numerous examples in the Gospel accounts where Jesus gathered large crowds around Him to observe His miracles and hear His teaching. Many pastors today use such texts as justification for using approaches to ministry that focus on drawing large crowds. Of course, at the end of Jesus' ministry, He ended up getting killed, which is typically not what popular pastors want for themselves. Nevertheless, the logic is that since Jesus performed miracles and fed the masses *so that* He could declare to them the good news of the Kingdom of God, so also, ministry leaders today can engage in ministry activities that will draw large crowds if this leads to people hearing the gospel message.

While there is nothing wrong in theory with this sort of ministry logic, the actual practices of certain ministries make one wonder if the goal of such crowd-gathering techniques is really to declare the gospel. It sometimes seems that the techniques used are instead focused on getting the church in the news. In fact, the methods used by some churches seem to actually contradict the gospel message, rather than support it. For example, I recently heard of one church that gave away a yellow Hummer during one of its gatherings. Not surprisingly, this particular church had record attendance at the event.

But is a Hummer giveaway really a reflection of the values of the Kingdom of God, or is it a reflection of the values of our materialistic and greedy society? And were the people really paying attention to what was being said from the pulpit, or were they anxiously watching the clock until the winning ticket number was called?

Regardless, one thing that is often missed by such appeals to the crowds that Jesus gathered is that by the end of Jesus' three years of ministry, these crowds were calling for His death. You will not find any "church growth" guru who says that this is the goal of drawing large crowds. Yet it is what happened to Jesus, and if Jesus is our guide, and this does not happen to us, then maybe we should reexamine what we say to the crowds who gather to hear us teach.

Acts 2

The primary text to defend pastoral popularity is Acts 2 and what happened to the early church on the day of Pentecost. On that day, after the Holy Spirit came upon the church, Peter preached a sermon and several thousand people were added to the church on one day. As the believers continued to live as followers of Jesus, thousands of others joined them. In just a few short weeks, the church went from 120 to over 5000 (Acts 4:4).

The argument is that since this happened with the early church, this is also what God wants to accomplish in our communities as well. Since the early church was born through exponential multiplication, the church that is doing what God wants will continue to grow in the same way today.

This sort of thinking is at the root of most modern church growth methodology. Today, church "growth" is defined not as transforming lives into fully-committed followers of Jesus Christ, but as getting as many bodies possible into the pews and onto the membership rolls.[1] Yet when the goal becomes large numbers, the primary task of the church moves away from leading people to live, love, and look like Jesus and instead focuses on getting more and more people to visit, attend, and give.

Sadly, it is this drive for exponential growth that causes so many problems in the church. When the focus becomes numbers rather than the people themselves, the church ceases to be a people of God following Jesus into the world, and instead becomes a business that maneuvers for greater market share. The church that focuses on the number of people that gather soon sees people not as other gifted people who serve alongside them in the ministry,

---

[1] See Jeremy Myers, *God's Blueprints for Church Growth* (Dallas, OR: Redeeming Press, 2020) for a longer explanation of biblical church growth principles.

but as conversions notched on a belt, statistics to report annually to the denomination headquarters, and metrics by which to judge which church in town is best.

The truth is that with the right techniques and enough financial backing, almost anyone can gather 10,000 people. But loving those the world hates, helping rescue someone from addiction, or showing people that they are loved by God is a spiritual victory which cannot be replicated, duplicated, systematized, or multiplied.

CONCLUSION

The examples of Jesus gathering crowds and what happened with the early church are not written in Scripture as examples to be followed for all Christians everywhere in every era. The ability to gather crowds is not the litmus test for whether or not God is blessing you and your ministry. Church is not a popularity contest.

Yes, sometimes crowds will gather. But sometimes (maybe most often) they will not, and we need to be fine with that. We need to focus not on the numbers but on the people already in our life, and how God might want to use us to help and encourage them and also what God might want to teach us through them. Since we are all the church, true church growth is not when the church grows in numbers, but when the church grows in looking and living more like Jesus.

The previous three chapters have considered the three pitfalls that pastors face in their ministry. These are pastoral pay, pastoral power, and pastoral popularity. All three keep pastors from performing the type of ministry they dream of and long for. But there is a way out. There is a solution. There is a way to accomplish the ministry you were called by God to perform. The next chapter reveals how this can be done.

DISCUSSION QUESTIONS

1. Do you think that you have an issue with seeking popularity? If so, why do you think this? What are some signs of this desire?

2. Do you feel the church has a hand in driving the pastor to desire bigger buildings, larger crowds, and more fame? Is this what the people in the pews desire as well?

3. Has your church performed activities that were labeled "evangelism" or "missions" that were really more about getting attention from others rather than giving love to them? How?

4. List of the activities and programs of your church. As you look through this list, what is the direction in which you want people to flow? In other words, in which direction do you want people to move? Are your programs geared toward getting people from the community into your church services, or are they focused on getting the people who already attend your church out into the community?

5. List the activities that your church performs on a regular basis that takes the people out of the church building and into the community. Now cross off the list any activity in which

church members invite people from the community to attend your church. Is there anything left on the list?

6. Has your church ever decided to spend money on the attractiveness or size of the building instead of on people? If so, what?

7. What is the thinking at the root of most church growth methodology? What is this the wrong focus?

CHAPTER 4

SAVING THE PASTOR

The previous three chapters considered the three primary pitfalls that pastors face in ministry. I wrote about them from personal experience. I have struggled with all three in my life. I knew I was gifted for pastoral ministry, and I wanted to be a pastor for my whole life, but I kept finding that the temptations of pastoral pay, power, and popularity kept me from doing the ministry to which God had called me.

But over a decade ago I discovered the solution to all three pitfalls. What is this solution?

I resigned as pastor.

This was the most liberating thing I had ever done as a pastor. I discovered that resigning as pastor liberated me to finally serve as a pastor in the way I had always wanted. Since that time, I have felt more like a pastor than ever before, and have found myself engaged in more pastoral ministry than I ever thought possible.

Let me share a bit more of my story with you, and in so doing, perhaps invite you to a whole different type of pastoral ministry, which may be the type of ministry you felt called to in the first place. I will share some of the benefits of resigning, and also suggest some ideas for how you can make a living away from professional, paid pastoral ministry.

Let me begin by saying that if you leave professional, paid, pastoral ministry, you will most likely miss several aspects of it. I was one who loved pastoral ministry. I loved the churches I worked in. I loved the people I worked with. Not a day goes by in which I do not desperately miss many elements of professional pastoral work. One of the reasons I left and (so far) have not gone back into full-time pastoral ministry is because of a conviction I have that I cannot get paid to be a pastor.

If you love pastoral ministry and you decide to leave, you will experience a similar sense of loss. If you found your identity in being a pastor, you might even experience some despair, depression, and feelings of uselessness. I have felt all of these.

However, as I find ways to fulfil my spiritual calling to be a pastor, even though I do not carry the title "Pastor" or get paid to do it, I have found that I am better able to engage in pastoral ministry with others than when I carried the title and got paid for it. Similarly, you may discover that resigning as pastor may actually help you become a better pastor. Your paycheck doesn't make you a pastor; God does. You are not a pastor because you are called "Pastor" by people, but because you actually pastor people. "Pastor" is a spiritual gift, and even though you may no longer be called "Pastor" by people you meet at church, or have the corner office, or get a paycheck for using your spiritual gift, you can still be a pastor, and maybe a better pastor than ever before.

For myself, I discovered that resigning as pastor actually freed me up to be a better pastor. When you are not a "paid" pastor, you no longer have to worry when attendance is low, or when tithing is down because several generous people in the church lose their jobs. You can preach and teach what God is showing you in Scripture without worrying if it will offend Mr. Moneybags, or if the church board will embark on a heretic hunt. Ultimately, you are freed to preach, teach, and disciple others as the Spirit leads and Scripture compels without the fear of losing your job or salary.

Furthermore, if you stay in the local church you are currently pastoring, and yet are not being paid to pastor, imagine the outreach and missional work you can accomplish in the community with the extra money the church now has (since they are not paying you)! As stated earlier, a recent study reported that the average pastor gets paid $84,000. Just think what this money could do for the hurting people in your town.

Not only could the church do more to serve and minister in the local community, but you, as the pastor, would also be freed up to pursue the ministry callings and desires God has laid upon your heart. Furthermore, when you find a job in the community to help pay your bills and provide for the needs of the family, you will be out "among the people," developing relationship and building friendships.

This is what exactly happened to me. Now that I am no longer being paid by a church to be the pastor, I work at a job in the local community. This job not only pays my bills, but it also puts me in touch with people who would never "attend" church. I am the "pastor" of the people at my worksite, even though they would never call me that. I seek to help them in life, speak words of encouragement, and, when asked for, provide biblical counsel and wisdom for life's problems. Surprisingly, I find that many of them "pastor" me as well, which is something I never had as a professional pastor.

Something similar can happen to you if you resign as pastor. Over time, you will begin to practice ministry the way you always dreamed it could be. If done right, resigning as pastor may just enable you to be a better pastor to your church and in your community, and to be the pastor God has truly called you to be.

BENEFITS OF RESIGNING AS PASTOR

There are numerous benefits to resigning as pastor. Five of these are described below.

No More Threat of Getting Fired

Professional "paid" pastors often live under the fear of getting fired. There are multiple reasons for this fear. Maybe they fear preaching something which the elder team disagrees with. Or perhaps they fear that some proposed change to a longstanding tradition will backfire. Sometimes, they simply fear that a personal conflict with some powerbroker or big donor in the church will lead to the church turning against them. Regardless of how it happens, pastors fear that their job and livelihood is at the mercy of the board or the big donors. I experienced all these fears when I was on the paid staff of a church. Maybe you have felt some of these fears yourself.

Sadly, some elders, board members, and big donors know that this fear exists, and use it to their advantage to get the pastor to do or say what they want. While most elder boards are filled with good and godly leaders, there are some that contain power brokers who like to control the church by constantly holding the threat of termination over the head of any pastor who tries to go against the will of the board.

In some churches, those who hold the purse strings control the pastor to do what they want by threatening him with salary cuts or worse yet, losing his job. Since the pastor depends on the church for income, some people use this to their advantage, threatening the pastor with loss of pay, or even loss of job, unless the pastor "comes around."

If you face these sorts of fears, imagine how liberating and freeing it would feel to never worry about such things again! If you resign as pastor, you will no longer face the fear of getting fired. You won't have to worry about whether or not you and the other elders agree on the direction of the church or how to allocate the budget.

None of this means, of course, that if you resign as pastor, you no longer need to seek the advice and counsel of others. You do. In fact, the decision to resign as pastor should probably be something you discuss with your board. Resigning as pastor does not free you from the necessity of seeking the wise input of others in the church. Instead, all it does is put everyone on a level playing field.

When the pastor resigns, he is no longer an employee. Instead, he becomes a co-laborer with the other elders. When pastors do not get paid for their services, the threat of not getting paid is no threat at all, and the pastor can now work with the board as one of its members. Resigning as pastor means that there is no more fear of getting fired.

No More Fear of Losing the Big Tither

Even if you get along fine with all the elders, threats could also come from a big tither in the church. Many churches around the country are not controlled by the board or by the pastor, but by the person in the church who gives the most money. Nobody wants to offend this person, because doing so might cause them to stop tithing or leave the church. As a result, everybody does whatever Mr. Moneybags wants.

This was my biggest concern when I pastored a small rural church. My concern turned out to be justified when I preached a sermon one Sunday that the big donor in the church disagreed with. He pulled his tithing and informed the church that he would not resume giving unless I resigned. I eventually had to resign. At the time, it didn't occur to me to stay on as the pastor, but gain my income from a local job. I ended up moving to another church. But to this day, I wish I had stayed in that community with that church.

Similarly, if you resign as a "paid" pastor, but stay on as pastor, you do not have to worry about offending Mr. Moneybags, because he is no longer paying your salary. You will no longer live in fear of someone with a fat wallet. You will no longer be controlled by the budget-master who writes your checks. Resigning as pastor liberates you from having to keep the big tither happy.

Redefine Pastoral Ministry

If you resign as pastor, you will have to find a job in the community to pay your bills (more on that later). But if you find a job and still want to remain a "pastor," it will be necessary to redefine "pastoral ministry."

Many pastors (as well as churchgoers) think that "pastoral ministry" only occurs in a church building and with church-attending people. But when a pastor comes to realize that God's church exists anywhere, at any time, and with any one, he can then become a pastor to all people, not just to the church-going people. It is only when a pastor recognizes this that true ministry really begins. A pastor who gets a job in the community quickly realizes he is a pastor not just to people who sit in pews on Sunday morning, but also to people who don't. He becomes a true "community pastor" not just a "church community pastor."

In the years since I left the paid pastoral ministry behind, I have found that my most fruitful and enjoyable pastoral ministry takes place over the fence in my backyard as I talk to my neighbor about his pear tree and help him get off his roof after his ladder fell down during a sudden rainstorm. Pastoral ministry takes place at my job when I talk with co-workers about their families and job stresses. Pastoral ministry takes place when I show a friend that God loves and accepts her, even though her parents say that God hates her. Pastors who resign from pastoral ministry often find that true pastoral ministry finally occurs when they are not getting paid to do it.

Other People Will Get Involved in Ministry

In the typical church, the pastor (or the pastoral team) does about 90% of the "ministry" functions of the church (however that is defined). But if the pastor has a job in the community, he has less available time for "church ministry." The pastor who works in the community can no longer spend 50, 60, or 70 hours a week on "pastoral ministry," which means that if he is going to partner with others, others will have to take over some aspects of the ministry.

In other words, the church might finally start to function like the Body of Christ that it is supposed to be, with each member doing its part (Eph 4:11-15).[1] As more people get involved, take

---

[1] See Jeremy Myers, *God's Blueprints for Church Growth* (Dallas, OR: Redeeming Press, 2020).

ownership, and help out with the ministry functions of the church, this contributes to the health of the church because more people are using their spiritual gifts and serving one another in love.

I am convinced that one of the main things holding people back from exercising their spiritual gifts in church is the presence of paid, professional, pastoral staff. People feel unqualified to serve in the church when there are seminary-trained pastors around who can do everything better. Sometimes the pastors feel this way too. But when the pastor can no longer do everything, the load must get shared and people must get involved. This is a good thing, as this is what God intended all along.

But what about the things that nobody else can do (or wants to do)? Honestly, if there is something that "only the pastor can do" then it probably doesn't need to be done. Many of the things that "only the pastor can do" were created by pastors over the centuries for the sake of job security. So if it is true that nobody else can do it, then just don't do it, and see what happens. If the church does not implode, crumble, or fail, then that pastoral function, whatever it was, did not need to be done. The church will continue to function on less paperwork, meetings, and programs, all of which is great for the health and vitality of the church. Resigning as pastor will liberate other church members to get move involved in ministry.

More Evangelistic Opportunities

Finally, finding a job in the community might also allow the pastor to become a member of the community. Pastors often pray for the opportunity to get to know the people of the town better. This prayer is easily answered by resigning from paid pastoral ministry to get a job in the community. When a pastor prays to get to know the community, God might answer this prayer by asking the pastor to resign. If this happens to you, follow God's leading with faith!

This is just good theology as well. By entering the community as a fellow worker, the pastor is following the footsteps of Jesus by incarnating himself among the people. This doesn't mean he can preach sermons or act all high and holy at the workplace. Nobody likes this, and some places will even fire people who try it. Instead, pastors in the community workplace can be pastoral simply by listening, watching, learning, and working hard. A pastor must be the best employee he can be.

Yes, there will be curse words and raunchy jokes. The pastor will learn things they didn't teach in seminary. But that's all okay. Though he's been to seminary, his true education begins the moment he steps away from paid, pastoral ministry. He will begin to understand why nobody ever cared to visit his church. He will discover that when he preached he was providing answers for questions nobody asked, and when he launched programs he was meeting needs nobody felt. When the church built that Sunday School wing, it spent money that could have been used elsewhere in the community.

Once a pastor begins to work in the community, he sees the true needs, questions, desires, fears, and pains that are out there. And once these are recognized, true love, service, and evangelistic opportunities multiply like never before. Being among the people, by the people, and for the people helps pastors love the people like Jesus.

These are just some of the numerous benefits to resigning as pastor. But let us now move to the number one problem that many pastors face when they consider whether or not to resign as pastor. What problem is that? It is the problem of how to make money.

HOW TO MAKE MONEY AFTER RESIGNING

The one big nagging question in the front of every pastor's mind is this: If I am no longer collecting a salary from the church, how am I going to make money? From where will I receive income?

Yes, this is a serious problem, isn't it? If you have considered leaving paid pastoral ministry, this is doubtless a question that you have been facing.

But the answer is simple: If you are no longer receiving an income from the church, you simply have to find another job. While it is true that by resigning from paid pastoral ministry you will not have to leave pastoral ministry, the reality is that you still need to receive income. So, you need to find a job.

Of course, while the answer is simple, actually *finding a job* is much more difficult. It can be difficult to find a job, especially one that fully replaces the salary you were receiving as a pastor. Furthermore, when you consider that most of your degrees, training, and experience is in the realm of Scripture and theology, the task of finding work can seem even more daunting. On the other hand, pastors often have good people, communication, and leadership skills, which makes them especially suited for a wide variety of jobs. But finding work can still be difficult.

When I left pastoral ministry, I applied for over 100 jobs, but was asked to come in for only two interviews. At one point, a Human Resource Manager was kind enough to tell me that they saw my education and experience as a sign that I was overqualified for the jobs I was applying for, and so they did not want to hire me because they thought that I would leave soon after I was hired. If you feel this might happen to you, it is not lying to simply leave some of your education off the application form, especially if your Bible training and seminary education are not applicable to the job for which you are applying. If you feel you must include all your education and earned degrees on your application, make sure you include in the application (and any interviews) an explanation about why you are looking for a second career so late in life.

In my situation, I did end up eventually landing a job. I became a carpet cleaner. It wasn't my ideal job, but it paid the bills. However, I had to quit after about six months because my body couldn't handle the job. I know this sounds silly, but I was working 80 hours each week, lost a lot of weight, and had two surgeries from injuries at work. I looked for a new job, and eventually found the position I have now. I have been here for over ten years and have no plans of leaving.

If you are thinking of resigning from the pastorate, I strongly suggest that you take steps to move in that direction, but don't quit your pastoral job without having another job lined up first. There are some who might tell you to "step out on faith" and quit your job, trusting God to provide, but I believe this is more foolish than faithful. But you can make your own decision.

If you choose to make the transition more slowly (or are having trouble finding a place that will hire you full time), you might be able to work something out with your church board where you work less at the church and find part-time work in the community. This has the added benefit of giving you some on-the-job training for a future career. If the board backs you in this decision, they should gladly provide you some time away from the church to prepare résumés, apply for jobs, go to interviews, or even attend schooling to get the education you will need to be better prepared for a "second career." Maybe some of the board members will even help you find a job. Remember to tell the board that with the money saved from your salary, the church can get more involved in loving others in the community.

Furthermore, if the board is aware of what you are doing, and you get a job where the pay is not comparable to what you were getting in the church, the church might consider supplementing your income while you gain more experience and knowledge and work your way up to a higher salary. This process may take a few years but the end result is worth the liberty and freedom that both the church and the pastor experience as a result.

But what type of job should you apply for? Well, to some degree, you almost need to go back to the days when you were in High School and the High School counselor helped you pick a career track. You need to figure out what you enjoy doing, what you are good at doing, what types of jobs are available, and how much money you need to make. All these factors are involved with finding a new job.

As I found out with my own job search, however, one difficulty we pastors have in finding a job outside the church is that all of our education and experience is frequently only with church. While many of us have lots of education and experience, it is only in the areas of Bible and Theology. There are not many businesses that are looking to hire someone with knowledge of Greek, Hebrew, and difficult-to-read theological terms.

However, if presented properly, many pastors have knowledge

and skills which many businesses are looking for: management and interpersonal skills being foremost among them. Also, one of the keys to running any business is communication and most pastors excel in communication skills. So on your job application and in your interviews, rather than talk about your theology degrees and how many sermons you preached, you might want to focus instead on your problem-solving skills, your ability to learn quickly, and your strengths in interpersonal communication.

Some pastors find that they excel in sales positions, customer service, and office management, while others do well in technical writing, editing, or teaching. Some pastors enter the financial industry, becoming bankers, brokers, accountants, or financial consultants. Many pastors become counselors at a high school or college, or even as a family and marriage counselor. For some reason, most of the pastors I know personally who have left the pastorate became salesmen. They sell cars, houses, insurance, clothing, home businesses, and timeshares. (I often wondered what it says about preaching that many pastors can take their powers of persuasive speech and apply them so easily to sales and marketing.) One area to seriously consider, and which will still use your pastoral experience and seminary education, is in becoming a prison, hospital, or military chaplain.

Lots of people in recent years are starting to make money online through selling training courses and digital products and services. Though it is not my full-time job, I myself have begun doing some of this as well through my website at RedeemingGod.com.

Regardless of the job you pursue, if you explain to your church what you are trying to do, it is quite likely that someone in the church knows of a job opening for which you are qualified.

If not, they might know something about resume preparation, or know someone in the Human Resources department at their workplace who can help you find a job in a local company or business.

GET SAVED AS A PASTOR

This chapter has been about how you, as a pastor, need to get saved.

No, not "saved" in the sense of receiving eternal life by faith in Jesus. You need to get "saved" in the sense of being rescued. Rescued from what? From the dangerous and damaging edifice that has been constructed around the pastoral position for the past fifteen hundred years.

You need to be freed from the expectations to do the work of the ministry while most of the congregation sits comfortably in their pews.

You must be delivered from the demands of having to live up to the phenomenal growth of the church down the street, the numerous books and television appearances of the pastor across town, and the power struggle in your own life and with the church board. A lot of this deliverance can be accomplished simply by resigning as pastor.

When you resign as pastor, you do not stop being a pastor, but simply decide to take steps so that you no longer receive a salary as a pastor.

Once this happens, there will be a significant decrease in the popularity contests and power games. The church will have more money for mission and outreach in the community and around the world. The people will learn that they are ministers also, and that following Jesus is more than just showing up on Sunday to hear a sermon and sing a few songs, but also involves loving each other and serving the world. In this way, you will save both yourself and your listeners. After all, when nobody is "the pastor," everybody becomes a minister, and the work of the ministry is shared by all.

This is what being the church is all about. This is true spiritual leadership. This is true pastoral ministry. This is how the role of pastor is redeemed. This is how the pastor is saved.

Are you ready to get saved? The rest of this book presents three other areas that will help save you, your ministry, and your church. We will look at some changes you can make in your preaching, in the church doctrinal statement, and in how the church prays. All of these areas can be saved, and you as the pastor can lead the way. Let us look at preaching first, and why we should simply stop preaching.

DISCUSSION QUESTIONS

1. What are some of the fears you have that hinder your ability to be the pastor you desire?

2. What would you miss most about full-time "paid" pastoral ministry if you resigned?

3. What types of ministry do you wish you had more time to pursue?

4. What types of services and mission's projects would your church like to accomplish, but does not have the money to complete?

5. What types of ministries could your church accomplish if 90% of the people were involved?

6. Do you think your church would be open to letting you slowly start seeking employment elsewhere for your income, while you continued to do certain aspects of your current pastoral ministry? This would, of course, require others in the church to step up and take over some responsibilities you currently handle. Would they be open to this?

7. Is there some way you could begin the process of less "church work" and more "pastoral work"?

8. What are some of the feelings you would have if you found yourself "freed" from your church obligations?

PART II: CONCLUDING THE SERMON

> *Christianity has become so self-righteous that I do not see much future in it. It wants to teach. It does not want to learn. It is arrogant. It is ... most interested in teaching people, but not in being taught by people.*
>
> —*Kosuke Koyama*

At the end of his Gospel, John writes that if all the things that Jesus did were written down one by one, not even the whole world could contain the number of books that would be written (John 21:25). Some days it seems that we are trying to see if John was right. Christian pastors and leaders often devote more time and energy to teaching, preaching, speaking, writing, and publishing than actually doing the things we teach and write about.

And here I am, writing another book about it. Of course, in general, I try not to just write about issues and ideas, but to write about things that I have actually put into practice in my own life. Writing, I believe, is not just about having something to say, but having something to live.

In Christianity, however, it seems that many authors would rather spend hundreds of hours and thousands of dollars writing about what Jesus said rather than actually doing what Jesus says. And much of this explanation of the words of Jesus seems to focus on explaining away the words of Jesus. We are experts at giving reasons why His words don't apply to us or wouldn't actually work except in an idealized world.

Do not misunderstand. I am not against writing and teaching about Scripture. I write and teach about Scripture almost every day. I think writing and teaching about Scripture is fine, as long as we have first put into practice what we write about. It is an issue of not putting the cart before the horse. In our teaching and writing, we must always work at maintaining the balance between opening the Bible in the study and applying the Bible in the streets. The true hermeneutical spiral is not simply an ever-tightening spiral as we circle in toward the true meaning of the text through deeper and more extensive study. No, truly seeking to understand Scripture also involves learning the text through trying to apply it in the world. One crucial element to Bible learning is Bible living. One cannot say they have understood the Bible and theology until they have learned to live it in their day-to-day lives. We are not just to know the Word, but are to live like the Word, that is, live like Jesus.

As pastors, we can lead others to live like Jesus rather than to just know about Jesus in many ways, but the one primary way we can lead others to follow Jesus is by showing them that it is okay to put down our Bibles, stop our studies, and go out into the world to put into practice that which we already know. We lead others to love, by actually *leading* them to love. If we only tell people to love, but we ourselves continue to study, teach, and preach, our example speaks louder than our words, and people will continue to learn and study rather than love and serve.

PART II: CONCLUDING THE SERMON 85

So pastor ... stop preaching and start loving. The following chapters will consider this radical idea in more detail.

CHAPTER 5

STOP PREACHING

I know that it seems nearly heretical to suggest that pastors stop preaching. After all, Jesus preached, Peter preached, Paul preached, and Timothy was commanded to "Preach the Word" (2 Tim 4:2). Furthermore, it is true, as many pastors claim, that American Christianity is a mile wide and an inch deep and we suffer from epidemic ignorance of the Scriptures. And yes, I believe that knowledge of Scripture is vital for faith and practice, and for knowing God and His will. I do believe in the importance and value of preaching and teaching.

But I also believe some other things.

I believe that far too many Christians think that before they can get out to love and serve others, they first need to know God and His Word better. And so they never get around to serving because they spend all their time studying.

I also believe that while growing in our knowledge of Scripture can be good and helpful, many modern preaching methods do not actually help people learn the Bible.

Furthermore, while I do believe that there is a direct correlation between how much Christians know and how much Christian love, the correlation is the opposite of what most people think. There is an inverse correlation between knowledge and love. It seems that in general, people don't love more as they learn more. Rather, those who know the most end up loving others the least.

This leads to the final thing I believe, which is that pastoral preaching and teaching is not God's only intended way—or even the primary way—of learning and living the Scriptures.

So while I do believe everything the Bible says about preaching and teaching and how pastors are to instruct and encourage other Christians to obey God's Word, I do not believe that the way preaching is often done today actually accomplishes its intended purpose. Preaching is not worth the time and energy that we put into it, and it doesn't seem to accomplish what we claim. Therefore, it might be best for pastors to simply stop preaching.

But aren't there numerous biblical passages which command pastors to teach and preach the Word of God? Aren't there numerous texts which provide examples of other men of God doing this very thing for the instruction, edification, and encouragement of the people of God? Yes, there are several texts which teach about preaching and provide examples of it. But these preaching texts say both more and less than what we think.

PREACHING TEXTS

As we consider several of the various texts below, watch for what is being said, to whom it is being said, why it is being said, and what terms the Bible uses to describe the entire process.

Nehemiah 8:8

In Nehemiah 8, the people of Israel gather in Jerusalem to hear Ezra read from the book of the Law of Moses. They did this on the first day of the seventh month, and Ezra read the Law from morning until midday (8:2-3). Verse 8 is often referenced as giving instructions on how to preach. The verse says that first the Law was read, and then someone gave the sense of the reading to help the people understand what was read.

Though this is often used as a great example of how to preach, what Ezra did in this text is not at all similar to modern preaching. First of all, the reason for the reading and explaining of the Law was because most of the Israelites had never heard it before (Neh 8:14). They didn't own copies of the Law, had never read it for themselves, and had never heard anyone read it or explain it to them. This is not true of most Christians today.

Second, this time of teaching was not a one-hour event which took place one day per week all year long, but was instead a three-to-four hour event which took place every morning for seven days in a row (Neh 8:3, 18). For one week the people gathered in the morning to hear the Law read and explained, and then in the afternoon, they would eat, drink, and celebrate (8:10-12).

Furthermore, it is highly debatable what form the teaching took. According to Nehemiah 8:7, numerous priests were involved. Most assume that these priests took turns teaching from the Law, but it is also possible that they had something like a panel discussion. Either way, the procedure does not look like our modern practice of one person doing all the talking.

The procedure, according to Nehemiah 8:8, was to begin with reading the Law of Moses. Does this mean that over the course of the week, they read through all five books of the Pentateuch, or does it mean just Leviticus? Did they read through it chapter by chapter, or did they approach it topically? How much did they read at one time? Who read it? We just don't know the answers to these questions, and so once again, we cannot equate it with the practice of reading a verse or two (or ten) before a sermon on Sunday morning.

Beyond the reading of the text, Nehemiah 8:8 says that they also gave the sense of the text. What does this mean? Most equate this with the modern form of preaching where the pastor explains what the text means and then provides some illustrations and application.

While this is possible, it is not likely. The Law was written in Hebrew, and since the generation of Israelites in view here had spent their entire lives in Babylon, a large number of them (if not the majority) probably did not speak Hebrew. So to "give the sense" likely means that after the Law was read in Hebrew, the priests translated it into the spoken language of the Israelites. Yes, it is possible that some additional explanation was provided by one or more of the priests, but the text does not say.

So if a church truly wanted to follow the pattern of Nehemiah 8, the first thing they would need to do is have the pastor stop preaching every week. Instead, the church should host an annual "Preach and Party" where for seven days the morning is reserved for studying a book of the Bible, and the afternoon for eating, drinking, and having fun together. A modern equivalent might be a one-week Bible teaching conference, in which the Bible is taught in the morning and then the people eat, drink, and socialize in the afternoons and evenings.

This form of preaching would consist of gathering several pastors together, and have one of them read from the Bible in Greek or Hebrew. After this, what was read must be translated into English, and possibly, if desired, the text can be explained. After the week was over, people would go home with the expectation that they put into practice the things they had learned that week. There also would be no further need to attend church or hear another sermon *for the rest of the year.*

Have you ever seen this sort of preaching done in churches today? While you might occasionally see pastors refer to the Greek or Hebrew, the passage is almost never read completely in Greek or Hebrew and then translated and explained. Even in the rare church that does have the pastor teach from the original languages, such sermons are never delivered by a panel of preachers, never for seven days in a row and then not at all the rest of the year, and never accompanied by a daily feast or celebration.

Frankly, this approach might benefit a lot of people and churches today. The people might learn more, the pastors would only preach in conversation with other pastors and only for one week out of the year, and every day would conclude with a big party. Many churches might really thrive from such a practice. I would love to see it happen, or even to participate. (Want to do it? Contact me!)

Regardless, whatever we get from Nehemiah 8, we do not find a pattern for the modern practice of preaching where one person gets up once a week for thirty to forty minutes, and gives a sermon. Nehemiah 8 is not prescribing what preaching must look like; it is describing what some Israelites did in a particular situation for a particular purpose. Many of those who were present had never heard the Law taught before, and so the Jewish scribes and teachers provided them with a week-long crash course on the teachings and requirements of the Mosaic Law. While this sort of practice might be helpful for new Christians or immature believers today, Nehemiah 8:8 does *not* provide is a description for how all pastors and Bible teachers today must proceed if they are to teach the Scriptures to others.

Isaiah 28:10-13

My preferred method of Bible teaching is book-by-book, verse-by-verse, line-by-line. This is also what I enjoy the most when I listen to someone else teach Scripture. I think that there are numerous benefits to this approach. It helps make the most sense of Scripture, provides the overall context of passages and hard to understand texts, and forces teachers to speak about things that they normally might skip over and avoid. Often, this style of preaching is referred to as "expository preaching."

Nevertheless, even though this is my preferred method of teaching, I am not sure we can say that it is the "biblical" model. But some say that it is, and they often use Isaiah 28:10-13 as proof. These verses talk about God's Word being taught line-by-line, word-by-word. While there are many other arguments to such a method of teaching which I personally find quite convincing, this verse does not prove that expository book-by-book preaching is God's preferred method.

First, it is important to recognize that there is some disagreement on how to translate verses 10 and 13. Traditionally, these verses have been translated "precept upon precept, precept upon precept, line upon line, line upon line, here a little, there a little" (or something similar). This is a decent translation of the words in these verses, but the context hints that something else is going on behind the mere meaning of the words. You can get a hint of this by reading how the Hebrew sounds: "*Saw lesaw saw lesaw, qaw leqaw qaw leqaw, ze'ir sham ze'ir sham.*" Even an English reader who does not understand Hebrew can hear how these words poetically roll off the tongue in a rhythmic and rhyming fashion.

Due to the rhythm of these words, several scholars believe that due to the surrounding context of these verses and what is going on in the passage, a better translation of these Hebrew words would be, "Blah blah blah, yada yada yada, same old same old" or some similar form or repetitive gibberish. But why would some Hebrew scholars desire to translate these lines in such ways? Because of the context.

The verses surrounding Isaiah 28:10-13 are crucial to properly understanding this text. In verses 5-6, God states what He wants to do in and through Israel. He desires to bring glory and beauty to His people. He wants justice to rule and strength to prevail. But there is a problem. According to verses 7-8, the rulers, the leaders, the priests, and the prophets have all become drunkards. They have no vision and their judgment is poor. All they do is wallow in their own vomit and filth.

When Isaiah tries to get them to learn the Law of God and reform their ways, they complain in verses 9-10 that the message of Isaiah is too repetitive and basic. They mock him by saying that he repeats himself and talks gibberish. They ridicule his teaching by summarizing it with the Hebrew words above, which as indicated, could be translated in the context as "Blah blah blah. Yada yada yada. Same old same old." They feel they have nothing to learn from Isaiah, that he repeats himself, and that his teaching is like the repetitive gibberish of babies.

How does God respond to this mocking criticism of Isaiah? In the following verses (Isa 28:11-13), God basically says, "So you claim you are not able to understand Isaiah, and that He speaks repetitive gibberish? Fine. I will give you gibberish. I will send the Assyrians who will speak to you in another language. I sent you

Isaiah so you would have refreshment and rest, but since you refused to listen to him, I will send you a people who will bring only death and destruction. You say you cannot understand Isaiah? You will really not be able to understand the Assyrians. Their speech will truly sound like 'Blah blah blah. Yada yada yada.'"

So does Isaiah 28:10-13 provide a good explanation of how God wants His Scriptures to be taught? Not even close. The statement about "precept upon precept, line upon line" is first of all a mocking statement by drunkards about the teaching of Isaiah, and then becomes a mocking statement by God as He turns their words back upon them. God tells them that if they don't understand Isaiah, just wait until the Assyrians arrive.

There is almost nothing in this text about how to preach and teach the Word of God. If there is anything int this text at all, it simply shows how Isaiah responded to the mocking words of the other Jewish leaders. Isaiah taught the same thing over and over and over in very simple words and ideas to the drunken leaders of Israel in hopes that through repetition and simplicity, they might understand his words and repent of their ways. But beyond that, this passage says nothing about God's approved method for preaching and teaching. We cannot use Isaiah 28 as a guideline for how to preach.

The Teaching Method of Jesus

What about the teaching method of Jesus? How did He teach, and what can we learn from it for our own teaching methods?

There are several forms of teaching we see from Jesus, and the Gospel writers only give much attention to one of them. As most pastors know, the form of teaching that the Gospel authors most frequently mention is Jesus' use of parables. Indeed, many pastors see the frequent use of parables by Jesus as a way to defend their own practice of telling stories in their sermons. It is not uncommon to hear pastors say, "Jesus told stories, and so should we." While there is nothing wrong with storytelling *per se*, there are three reasons that sermons filled with stories are not a proper imitation of Jesus' teaching style.

First, while there is no denying that Jesus told stories, His stories were not *just* stories. They were parables. And the parables of Jesus were *not* told in order to reveal and illustrate truth, but to conceal and hide it. Jesus spoke in parables to keep most of the people confused, not to help explain or illuminate the truth. How do we know this? Because this is what Jesus said. In Luke 8, after Jesus told one of His parables, the disciples did not understand what He was talking about and so asked Jesus why He spoke in parables. He responded by saying that He speaks in parables "So that in seeing, they will not see, and in hearing, they will not understand" (Luke 8:10). In other words, Jesus spoke in parables *to hide or mask the truth*.

There are numerous reasons why Jesus did this. In some cases, Jesus only wanted the truth to be known by those who were ready to receive it. In other cases, He wanted to further develop the relationship He had with His disciples when they asked Him what His parables meant. The parables of Jesus revealed truth to those who were ready to hear it, but masked the truth from those who were not ready. These parables still function this way today.

Beyond this, however, Jesus often taught without parables at all. Most people do not realize it, but the vast majority of Jesus' weekly teachings are not recorded anywhere in Scripture, and it appears that in most of these teachings, He did not use parables.

The Gospels record that every week on the Sabbath, Jesus

could be found in the synagogue, teaching those who had gathered (cf. Luke 4:14-16, 31; 6:6; 13:10). If Jesus followed the pattern of other Jewish Rabbis at the time, He would have read a text of Scripture and then explained it in detail, while answering questions or objections from the other members of the synagogue (cf. Luke 4:17-27). Regrettably, other than the few brief comments in Luke 4:20-27, not a single one of these synagogue Scripture teachings of Jesus are recorded in the Gospels.

Furthermore, in the typical Sabbath-day synagogue meeting, when one Rabbi finished teaching, the people were not dismissed to go home. Instead, another Rabbi would often take a turn at teaching. It was not uncommon to have between five and seven such teaching sessions every Sabbath in the local synagogue, with different Rabbis teaching different portions of Scripture. In such a way, they taught through the Pentateuch (the first five books of the Bible) in about three years. If Jesus followed this pattern, as it appears that He did, then He would have performed this teaching every Saturday for at least three years. And since Jesus' goal in such settings was to simply and clearly explain the text rather than hide the meaning of the text, it seems unlikely that Jesus used parables in this context.

But even these two forms of teaching—His use of parables for the uninformed masses and antagonistic religious leaders, and His use of clear Bible teaching in the Synagogue on the Sabbath—were not the only two forms of teaching Jesus used. He also frequently taught His disciples in intimate, small-group settings (cf. John 14–16). In these settings, Jesus almost never used parables, nor did He provide formalized teaching from Scripture. Instead, He answered questions and engaged in dialogue with His disciples about the issues they were facing. His specific teaching to His disciples was clear, concise, and spoke directly to their concerns.

So it is simply untrue to say that "Jesus always spoke in parables, and so should we." Jesus only spoke in parables when He wanted some of His listening audience to be confused about what He was saying. His regular, weekly teaching in the Synagogue consisted of a clear and systematic explanation of the Torah. He also clearly and concisely answered the pressing questions and concerns of His disciples.

Does any of this help pastors today know how they should preach and teach? Maybe. But before we consider that question, let us look at how the Apostles preached.

The Teaching Method of the Apostles in Acts

When people think of the teaching method of the Apostles, they often think of the sermon by Peter on the Day of Pentecost in Acts 2:14-39, or that of Stephen in Acts 7 right before he was stoned to death. But both of these events are not examples of the primary teaching method of the Apostles. Rather, both cases are extemporaneous explanations to an unbelieving audience about what was happening in their midst. People had questions about what was happening, so Peter and Stephen answered these questions. These were not prepared messages for the purpose of edifying and instructing the people of God.

Many of the messages of Paul in Acts are similar. For example, Acts 17:22-31 is not formal teaching, but is a logical presentation to a gathering of philosophers in which Paul argued for the existence of the one, true God and the resurrection of Jesus from the dead. It is not an interactive discussion of a biblical text for the instruction and edification of other believers. Instead, Paul is addressing the questions and issues of local, unbelieving philosophers as a way to introduce them to the good news about Jesus Christ.

And while these types of teaching do receive the most attention in the Book of Acts, they were not the method of teaching that was most frequently used by the Apostles. The method the Apostles most frequently used was similar to the method Jesus most frequently used.

It appears that the teaching method of the Apostles followed the method of Jesus. Using books of the Bible as their primary texts, and following a set pattern, one person would read the text in Hebrew, and another would interpret it into Greek, and then the text would be explained and applied (cf. Acts 2:42; 13:14-15; 14:1-3; 15:21; 18:4; 19:8-10; etc.). John Lightfoot records that the one who interpreted from Hebrew to Greek was called "an interpreter," and the teaching as an "interpretation" (cf. 1 Cor 12:10; 14:26).[1] The regular times of teaching were often done in the homes of followers of Jesus, and were usually accompanied by a meal and prayer (Acts 2:42).

One example of this is found in Acts 20:7-11, where Paul delivers an extended explanation of Scripture to some gathered believers. The text says that Paul "continued his message until midnight" (20:7) and "Paul continued speaking" (20:9). Of course, there is no mention of what Paul was speaking about, but this was taking place on Sunday with other followers of Jesus, and was accompanied by a meal (20:7). And while we cannot be certain, the topic of this message was probably about the proper interpre-

---

[1] John Lightfoot, *Commentary on the New Testament from the Talmud and Hebraica* (Peabody, MA: Hendrickson, 1989), 68.

tation and application of biblical texts in light of the revelation of Jesus Christ. Paul consistently taught about Jesus Christ and Him crucified (1 Cor 2:2), so there is no reason to think this time of teaching would be anything other.

Of course, even here, Paul was not delivering a monologue. The word used in both Acts 20:7 and 20:9 for the "message" and "speaking" of Paul is *dialegomai*, which is the root Greek word behind the English word, "dialogue." Paul was not the sole speaker for hours on end, but was instead engaged in an interactive discussion or debate with others who were present (cf. the same word in Acts 17:17; 18:4, 19; 19:8-9).

So even with the apostles, we see various forms of teaching being used in various situations and contexts. The most formalized teaching, and the most consistent, however, involved clearly and systematically explaining the Scriptures to a group of believers on a regular basis. Even these times of teaching were not like sermons of today, however, but were closer to what we would call a "Bible Study" where people could raise questions and provide their own input on the passage being discussed. There is nothing anywhere in the Book of Acts that resembles the modern Sunday sermon monologue.

CANCEL THE SERMON

As a result of this brief survey of a few key Scripture passages about preaching, we have learned something surprising. We have learned that even though most people assume that preaching consists of one person standing on a stage (often behind a pulpit) to deliver a monologue about a biblical text or topic for 20-40 minutes while everyone else listens, such a practice is not found anywhere in Scripture (see Appendix I). In other words, there is no biblical basis for the modern practice of the monologue sermon.

What this means is that you can cancel your sermon if you want to. Since there is not one passage in the Bible that commands (or even describes) the modern practice of delivering a monologue sermon once a week to a crowd of gathered people, you don't need to do it if you don't want to.

But there is no prohibition against it either. This means that if you have good reasons for continuing to offer a 30-40 minute monologue sermon on a topic or passage that is instructive and helpful to the people in the audience, then there is no reason to stop the practice. Since the practice is neither commanded nor condemned, the practice can be either cancelled or continued.

But how are we to decide?

Since the pastor is the shepherd over the flock of God, each pastor (or pastoral team) is to decide which activities are most beneficial for the people under their care. Pastors are to guide, lead, direct, feed, and protect the people in their own flock. Therefore, if the pastoral team is convinced that a regular Sunday sermon is the best use of time and energy to help people live more like Jesus, then they should make the Sunday sermon a priority. Even though the Bible does not contain any indication that Jesus and the Apostles practiced anything like our modern Sunday sermon monologue, this does not mean that the modern practice is wrong. Rather, there may very well be a place for such sermons in today's Christianity. But if we are going to provide a weekly Sunday sermon, we must also provide good reasons for such a practice.

What other reasons could there be? There are numerous possible reasons why a pastor or church leader may decide to give monologue messages. Maybe a monologue sermon is the best way to instruct and encourage many people all at once. Perhaps Sunday sermons are the best way to spread a visionary message quickly to the people. Maybe for the group you are working with, listening to a monologue is their primary learning style. It is for these reasons that educational centers provide large-group learning session, and many political leaders hold large-scale rallies. There are many good reasons to provide large-event teachings to Christians.

In my current job as a prison chaplain, I provide sermons every week, but this is because the Sunday sermon is the only chance I get during the week to speak truths of love, grace, and forgiveness into the lives of people who know almost nothing of such things. For most of these men, the Sunday service is the only time I have to present such truths to them. And while I have tried incorporating interaction and dialogue into these prison services, the nature of prison makes such a practice nearly impossible. So in order to provide good, sound doctrine to people who have never heard such things before (and might not ever again), I rely on a weekly Sunday sermon to help spread the message of the gospel as far as possible.

You might have similar sorts of reasons for providing a Sunday sermon. But you can think of no good reason to preach a Sunday sermon on a regular basis, there is no reason to continue to the practice. Since there is no command for the practice in Scripture, you have permission to cancel the Sunday sermon and set your people free to follow Jesus into the world. Maybe you will still want to provide a monthly sermon, or a yearly sermon, but whatever you offer, make sure you maintain your goal of shepherding the flock of God.

And regardless of which way you teach others and lead others to follow Jesus, please recognize that there is no such thing as "one right way." The way you are preaching and teaching is not the *required* way, and the way the pastor across town is preaching and teaching is not necessarily the wrong way. Any way can be the "right" way if it truly leads people to look and act like Jesus in this world. If we are going to properly preach and teach today, we must find ways to preach and teach that effectively accomplish this purpose.

If you can lead people to live like Jesus without preaching and teaching several times a week, then you should feel the freedom to do so. The goal of the pastor is to provide healthy teaching, however that looks.

HEALTHY TEACHING

In the previous section, I frequently mentioned that there was no command in Scripture to regularly provide a Sunday sermon. As you read these claims you might have had questions about 2 Timothy 4:2, in which Paul instructions Timothy to "Preach the Word." Paul goes on to tell Timothy that a time will come when people will not want to listen to sound teaching. You might think I am guilty of fulfilling this prophesy when I tell pastors that they don't have to provide sermons if they don't see the need for them. But is this really what 2 Timothy 4:2 says? No, it is not.

Second Timothy 4:2 is typically used in two ways. This text is sometimes used to explain why some people don't want to attend church and listen to a sermon. But the second, more popular, way this verse is used is when a small-church pastor wants to criticize a mega-church pastor. Often, small-church pastors who "preach the Word" will criticize mega-church pastors for having crowded pews and empty sermons. They say, "Well, that pastor is just giving fluff sermons, but people go there because they want their ears to be tickled. As Paul said, 'they will gather around them teachers who give them what their ears want to hear.'"

But what does the verse mean? The first thing to consider is *why* Paul exhorted Timothy to continue proclaiming the good news about Jesus in the first place (2 Tim 4:2). In Paul's day, as in our own, most people did not want to receive "sound doctrine" or "good teaching." Then, as now, most people only heard what they wanted to hear.

In fact, when Paul writes about a time in which people will turn away from the truth and gather around themselves false teachers who give them what their itching ears want to hear, he was not making a prediction about a far-off future event, but something that was already happening to the people under Timothy's care. The context reveals this to be the case.

For example, the vice list in 2 Timothy 3:1-9 says that "In the last days ... men will be ..." and then goes on to list certain traits that have been in existence among all people since the beginning of time. So when Paul writes about "the last days," he is not thinking about some future event, but their *own* days. There were clearly people in Timothy's congregation (as in all congregations) who were lovers of themselves, lovers of money, boasters, proud, etc. There were people like this in the days of Moses (2 Tim 3:8), there will be people like this in the future, and there were people like this in Paul's own day as well. In fact, after his exhortation to Timothy in 4:1-5, Paul describes some individuals who have forsaken him out of love for this present world (2 Tim 4:10). So Paul's description of people gathering to hear false teachers is not a description of something that will happen in *future* generations, but is a description of what happens in *every* generation. Are there people today who fit Paul's description? Yes, there are; just as there were such people in Paul's day.

What is the Warning?

But what exactly is the warning? Who are the people who do not want to listen to sound doctrine? Is it the people who attend mega-churches to listen to "fluff sermons?" Is it the people who don't attend church at all because they don't like sermons? Or maybe it is someone like me who says that sermons generally aren't needed today! What is this "sound doctrine" that people reject? How can we make sure we do not fall into the trap of rejecting sound doctrine?

To begin with, it must be noted that the phrase "sound doctrine" would be better translated as "sound teaching" or "healthy teaching" (Gk., *hugianousa didaskalia*). In Luke 5:31, 7:10, and 15:27, *hugianousa* refers to healthy bodies that function properly, and so when the word is applied to doctrine, it means something similar.

For example, 1 Timothy 1:10 uses the same Greek phrase (Gk., *hugianousa didaskalia*) in contrast to homosexuality, kidnapping, lying, and perjury. Such things are not doctrinal beliefs, but lifestyle behaviors. Therefore, "sound doctrine," or healthy teaching, is better understood as the opposite of such behaviors, which would be good and godly behaviors. Also, in Titus 1:9 the phrase is used in the context of proper behavior, such as hospitality, holiness, justice, and self-control (Titus 1:8). Paul also shows that good teaching leads to sound doctrine, which is seen in people who are temperate, respectable, self-controlled, and loving (Titus 2:1-2). So the phrase *hugianousa didaskalia* doesn't refer to proper beliefs, but to proper behaviors that are in line with Jesus Christ.

In fact, when a biblical author wants to use *hugianousa* in connection to beliefs and teachings, he connects it with the Greek word for *word* (Gk., *logos*) as in 1 Timothy 6:3, and 2 Timothy 1:13, rather than with *didaskalia*. So once again, the best way to understand *hugianousa didaskalia* is in connection to healthy teaching that is best seen through righteous and holy living. It does not primarily refer to good beliefs or sound theology.

Healthy teaching is not necessarily a form of preaching that proclaims the gospel every week and invites people to "come forward." Nor is it necessarily a form of teaching that digs deep into the Hebrew and Greek words of the text, quotes Augustine and Calvin, and uses big theological words. Healthy teaching definitely has nothing to do with whether or not you agree with the theological positions of the pastor down the street or how many people he packs into his pews on a Sunday morning. None of these things are indicative of healthy teaching, or the lack thereof.

No, in the immediate and wider context of Scripture, healthy teaching is that which encourages a person to enter into the world and live like Jesus among the people of the world. Healthy teaching is teaching that focuses on helping people follow Jesus in loving service to the world. Healthy teaching sees love, service, and action in the world as the ultimate goal. In a healthy teaching environment, you know you have learned it if you do it.

In contrast, unhealthy teaching is the kind of teaching that causes people to withdraw from the world. Unhealthy teaching results only in condemnation and judgment of the world. Unhealthy teaching focuses more on *learning about Jesus* while not caring so much about *becoming like Jesus*. Unhealthy teaching sees knowledge and learning as the goal. In an unhealthy teaching environment, you know you have learned a text if you can recite and regurgitate it.

Therefore, who are those that follow teachers who give them what their itching ears want to hear? They are those who are content to gather more and more teachers, listen to more and more sermons, gain more and more Bible knowledge, and become so busy with Bible study, theological learning, and the accumulation of spiritual trivia, they never get around to putting any of it into practice in the world. Unhealthy teaching is that which results only in more teaching. Those who gather around themselves teachers who give them what their itching ears want to hear are those who love to listen to sermons, read theology books, and attend Christian conferences, while rarely putting any of it into practice in the world. They accumulate teachers and teachings, but never live out what they learn.

This is Paul's point in 2 Timothy 4. Paul wants Timothy to lead his church away from simply wanting to get more and more teaching, and instead take them out into the world where they can proclaim the gospel by loving and serving others, just as Jesus did for us. Paul encourages Timothy to provide and encourage people toward healthy teaching that results in action and putting into practice what is learned.

Unhealthy Teaching in the Church

Now that we see the difference between healthy teaching and unhealthy teaching, which of the two is more prominent in many churches today? That is, are people most concerned with gaining more Bible knowledge, listening to more sermons, accumulating more Bible facts, attending more Bible studies, and sitting through more Bible seminars? Or, are they more concerned with taking what they already know and going out into the world to put it into practice? Statistics and experience show that it is typically the former.

While there is often an exhortation at the end of a sermon or Bible study for people to go out and put into practice what they have learned, the schedule and programs of the church reveal that what is most important is faithful attendance on Sunday morning so that one can learn about the Bible in Sunday School, learn about the Bible during the sermon, and learn about the Bible in a mid-week Bible study. In most church settings, those who are really "mature" will take copious sermon notes, study the Bible on their own for an hour or two every day, and listen to sermons on the radio while driving to work. They will download MP3 sermons from the internet for listening while jogging or weeding the garden, read theology books in their spare time, and attend one or two Bible conferences every year.

If you ever suggest to such a person that maybe they know enough about the Bible and maybe they should start putting some of it into practice, they will either stare at you like you are speaking another language, or they call you a heretic for downplaying the centrality of Scripture.

I know because I was one of those types of Christians. I listened to sermons every chance I had, read books only about the Bible, and could only have discussions with people if they talked about the Bible. My primary interests were the newest interpretation of a tough biblical text, the greatest insight into a unique

Greek word, or the best explanation of a theological debate. I traveled across the country to listen to various teachers, attend popular conferences, and scoured the internet to understand new theological developments. I gathered around myself thousands of books, CDs, tapes, and MP3 files of all the best preachers and teachers, as well as two full four-drawer filing cabinets of articles and sermons notes.

While I was doing all this, I thought of it as "preparing for ministry." Once I was in "the ministry," I thought of my never ending quest for more Bible knowledge as "sharpening my skills," "increasing my knowledge," "meditating on the Word," or having "iron sharpen iron." This quest for knowledge consumed my time and energy so that I barely had any left for any of the people in my life. My wife and family were always neglected and I barely knew the names of my neighbors. In my attempt to prepare for the ministry and become the best minister possible, I failed to love or serve the people who were closest to me in life.

I now believe that I was trapped by the unhealthy teaching that Paul had in mind. I was enslaved to the type of teaching where the only goal is more teaching. I was part of a large group of Christians who had itching ears for more teaching, and to satisfy this desire, we gathered around ourselves a whole host of teachers who promised to fill our days, weeks, and months with the best biblical teaching that existed. But all the while, our lives went unchanged, love was not shown, generosity was not practiced, care was not given, forgiveness was not offered, and peace was not produced. Though we thought we were the healthiest Christians of all, we had become victims of unhealthy teaching.

This is what Paul warned Timothy about in 2 Timothy 4:1-4. Unhealthy teaching is when we heap up for ourselves more and more teachers, sermons, Bible studies, and conferences. It is being so excited about what we heard, that we cannot wait to hear more. And after we hear more, our primary response is an excited expectation to hear even more. Unhealthy teaching is the teaching that only results in more teaching. As great as Scripture study can be, it can also become an addiction. Bible study can actually become like a drug that pulls us away from the God of the Bible. The more we study the Bible, and the more we learn about God, the less we end up obeying the Bible and following God. Sometimes you have to give up your commentaries and word studies so that you can actually hear what God is saying and follow him, not deeper into the text, but deeper into the sin and darkness of this world.

While the ears of some people do itch for funny stories, jokes, and encouraging insights based on psychology and current events, the ears of other people itch to hear the latest insight on a difficult Bible passage, or the newest scholarly explanation of a particular word in Scripture. This second group attends Bible studies, listens to expositional preaching, buys commentaries, does word studies, learns Greek and Hebrew, and all the while, looks down their noses at people who don't do such things.

According to Paul, neither group is better than the other. What God wants is that we go and make disciples, which does not mean teaching people everything there is to know about Bible and theology, but leading people to live like Jesus within the world. Making disciples means much more than filling people's heads with expert knowledge of Scripture. It requires more than teaching, preaching, and Bible Study. Making disciples means making people self-feeders of Scripture, encouraging them to practice what they learn, and giving them the freedom to follow

Jesus into the world. All of that does not necessarily require a Sunday service with songs and a sermon.

The Solution

Since this is so, we can no longer accuse pastors and churches of teaching unsound doctrine and of gathering around themselves a heap of teachers who tell them what their itching ears want to hear simply because they disagree with our theology or because we don't like their style of preaching. It is not so much about their preaching method or even the theology they preach.

I often hear these sorts of accusations coming from various pulpits in the United States. When I was a pastor I made a few such accusations of my own. "They just tell a bunch of stories; but we teach the Bible. Their sermons are full of psycho-heresy; but we have sound doctrine. They water down the gospel; we preach it fully."

Ironically, whenever pastors warn their people about falling away from sound doctrine, the solution is always to attend church more regularly, get plugged into a weekly Bible study, read Christian books, listen to Christian radio, and study the Bible on their own every day. It appears that this sort of prescription might be the exact thing that Paul was warning others against in 2 Timothy 4:1-4—the teaching that only results in more and more teaching. In warning people against "unsound doctrine" many modern pastors end up promoting it.

Therefore, the prescription for unhealthy teaching is not in obtaining greater teaching and more learning, but rather, less teaching and more living. The teaching that Paul desires is the teaching that does not take people away from the world, but into it; not away from people, but among them; not away from the questions and troubles of life, but toward them. Healthy "teaching is not with a speculative soteriology slanted away from the world but with true, rational and proper life in the world."[2] Healthy teaching does not deal with the lofty ideas, the theoretical explanations, or the speculative theology which so many pastors and Christians are fond of hearing. No, healthy teaching takes seriously the gospel announcement of Jesus that the Kingdom of God is at hand, and gets our noses out of the Bible and into the streets and stores of our cities.

The world is not renewed and the gospel is not spread through ideas and preaching only, but also through putting the ideas and values of the gospel into deed and action. Healthy teaching is the teaching that results in loving and serving others. As Christoph Blumhardt said, "Jesus does not want to renew the world through ideas, but through deeds."[3] In this way, we will truly be practitioners of sound doctrine and healthy teaching.

CONCLUSION

This chapter has issued an invitation to stop preaching. And now you see why. If the way you are preaching is not tangibly making people more like Jesus, then you don't need to do it any longer. You should always invite people to live in light of the good news about Jesus, but it may very well be that the Sunday sermon is no longer the best way to accomplish this. It might be that the people under your care already know enough, and they simply need

---

[2] Ulrich Luck, "hugianō" in *Theological Dictionary of the New Testament* (Grand Rapids: Eerdmans, 1972), VIII:312.
[3] Christoph Blumhardt, *Action in Waiting*, 131.

to be led into living out what they already know.

Maybe we need to put down our Bibles and pick up a shovel and a rake, or soap and a towel, or a pot and ladle, and go out and put into practice what we already know. In this way, we will be healthy students of the Word (See Appendix I for more on this topic). Rather than continue to learn the Scripture, it might be time to start living the Scriptures. This is the topic of the next chapter.

DISCUSSION QUESTIONS

1. Define preaching in your own words.

2. What is different about modern preaching methods and what we read about in Nehemiah 8:8?

3. What is Isaiah 28:10-13 describing? Is it a principle for modern preaching? Why or why not?

4. Why can we not use the parables of Jesus as a model for modern preaching?

5. What did Jesus' weekly teaching in the synagogue probably look like?

6. What is "sound doctrine" or "healthy teaching"?

7. What are the results of healthy teaching?

8. What are the results of unhealthy teaching?

9. What does it look like to "gather around teachers for themselves who give them what their itching ears want to hear"?

10. What are some possible ways for pastors to provide "healthy teaching" for their people?

CHAPTER 6

LIVING THE SCRIPTURES

The previous chapter suggested that it is okay to stop preaching. When pastors hear this suggestion, they often raise numerous objections and questions. For example, how are people to learn Scripture, if not through preaching? How can people learn to obey God, if someone doesn't teach them what Scripture says and how to live in obedience to it?

This chapter seeks to answer these sorts of questions. In it, we will see that learning the Scriptures is more about living and following them than memorizing and studying them. Certainly, reading, studying, and thinking about Scripture is an essential part of learning the Bible, but I am convinced that until we learn to live the Scriptures, we have not learned them.

In other words, the Scriptures are not just a means by which God imparts information to human beings about Himself, our present situation, and how to get into a right relationship with Him. Yes, the Bible contains truths about these things, but simply learning these facts is not the primary goal and purpose of Scripture.

The primary goal and purpose of Scripture is related to the primary goal and purpose of God for this world: He wants to create a people for Himself who can be His representatives on earth.

God wants a people who will be His hand, feet, and voice to this world. He wants a people who will be His incarnation. We learn and live the Scriptures, not by sitting in a room, reading the Bible, and discussing with others what it says, but by getting out into the world and living like Jesus among others.[1]

By looking at what the Bible says regarding preaching and teaching, we have learned that the 30-minute Sunday sermon is not as critical as we make it out to be. It is not worth the time and energy we often give it, especially when compared to the things that the pastor and the people of the church *could* be doing in the community instead. In general, most Christians already know enough about the Bible. They don't need to learn more; they simply need to put into practice what they already know. The following chapter looks at how this can happen, and how the pastor can lead the church to make it happen. Rather than seeing ourselves as dispensers of biblical truth, we must start viewing ourselves as disciplemakers, who lead others into biblical apprenticeship to Jesus.

BIBLICAL APPRENTICESHIP

Throughout most of Scripture—beginning with God in the Garden of Eden with Adam and Eve, carrying on through Moses and the Prophets, and all the way to Jesus and the Apostles—the primary method for teaching was something I call "On the Way Teaching." This teaching was similar to what we think of as "ap-

---

[1] Jacques Ellul, *The Subversion of Christianity* (Grand Rapids: Eerdmans, 1986), 199.

prenticeship." In fact, rather than thinking of biblical preaching and teaching, it might be best to think of biblical apprenticeship as the best model for learning the Scripture and putting them into practice.

Jesus provided an excellent model for how this type of learning looked. He invited twelve men to be His Apprentices, and as they followed Him around in His ministry, they watched what He did, asked questions about how and why He did it, and tried to accomplish similar tasks that were assigned to them by Jesus. While there were probably some times of formal teaching, it seems that most of the instructional times were either on the way to a place where Jesus would minister, or on the way back from ministering. He was either preparing His disciples for what they were about to do, or was debriefing them about what had just happened.

In this way, the teaching was need-centered and issue-focused. On the way to ministry, He told them what they needed to know to love and serve others. On the way back from ministry, He answered their questions about why things hadn't gone as planned and what could be done in the future. In this way, teaching involved both learning and doing, and the learning was always extremely focused on what it was they were doing.

Though nearly every teaching of Jesus follows this pattern, a few examples from the Gospels are helpful. At one point in His ministry, Jesus sent out the twelve disciples to put into practice the things they had learned (Luke 9:1-10). After they returned, He provided further teaching and instruction about discipleship, and then sent them out again (Luke 10:1-16). When they return the second time, they report what happened, and once again, Jesus provides further instruction. Around this same time, the disciples also try to cast out a demon and are unsuccessful. When they ask Jesus why they were unable to help this demon-possessed man, Jesus provides further instruction on casting out demons (Matt 17:14-21).

As can be seen, the disciples were not just learning for the sake of learning, but were learning for the purpose of immediately putting into practice what they had learned, or were learning more about something they had just done. In this way, teaching was nearly always "on the way." It was done while on the way to do a ministry, or on the way back from ministry. It prepared the disciples to love, serve, and give, or it answered the questions they had regarding problems and issues they had faced while loving or serving others. For Jesus, doing what was taught was just as important as hearing it. Learning the Scriptures and what God's plan is for the world requires both hearing what the Scriptures say and putting the Scriptures into practice. But that is exactly the problem. Learning the Scriptures is one thing; practicing them is quite another.

THE LACK OF PRACTICE

Many pastors, priests, and professors agree that the big problem in the church today is that no matter how much a person knows about the Bible, few of us actually live out what we know. The vast majority of Christians, whether they know a lot about the Bible or hardly any at all, fail to put into practice the little (or lot) that they already know. This means that the problem in the church is not necessarily a lack of learning, but a lack of practice. And the problem is only getting worse.

Yet for the last several decades, the only proposed solution to this problem is that pastors should provide more and better teaching. Some focus on more teaching, so that they teach Sunday morning, Sunday night, and Wednesday night. It is believed that more preaching will lead to better Christians. These pastors also tend to believe that the sermons should be longer and more biblically based.

Other pastors, however, believe that it is not the quantity of sermons that matter, but the quality. It is also not as necessary for people to know the chapter and verse of biblical truths as it is to know the biblical truths themselves. Furthermore, they know that their sermons are competing with television, sports, and iPhones, and so they try to make their sermons as interesting and fast-paced as possible. They sprinkle their sermons with colorful anecdotes, emotional stories, and video clips from the latest movies. The argument is that before people can practice the Bible, they must be interested in learning what it says. Our sermons, therefore, must first and foremost be interesting.

But none of it seems to be working.

The studies have been done, the statistics have come in, and the books have been written.[2] Christians typically do not act better than their non-Christian neighbors, and in many cases, act worse. Because many of us Christians feel that we have "the truth," we tend to set ourselves up as the moral policeman of the world (even though we ourselves are not that moral), and only

---

[2] See, for example, David Kinnaman & Gabe Lyons, *unChristian* (Grand Rapids: Baker, 2012); George Barna, *The Second Coming of the Church* (Nashville: Thomas Nelson, 2001); David Kinnaman, *You Lost Me* (Grand Rapids: Baker, 2016).

come across to others as hypocritical and hyper-judgmental. It seems that all our preaching and teaching is not achieving the intended purpose.

So maybe the solution is not that we need more and better teaching, but less and more intentional teaching. What if the problem has nothing to do with the preacher, how long we preach, the illustrations we use, the structure of the sermon, or how much we focus on the text? What if the problem is with preaching itself? What if we don't need to fine-tune our preaching, but can simply discard it? Could it be that preaching is not the cure for biblical illiteracy and a lack of biblical living, but the cause? Could it be that a dependence upon pastors to provide sermons and Bible studies is what actually leads to the widespread failure to live and love like Jesus?

If the answer to any of these questions is "Yes," then what we need is not more preaching, but less. Maybe what we need is not to remind people of how much they do not know, but instead to point them to the few things they already know, and then lead them to live out these things in their daily lives among the people they interact with. When approached this way, less biblical teaching might actually lead to more biblical living, and in this way, end up with higher biblical literacy than ever before.

RAISING BIBLICAL LITERACY

Yes, it is a problem that people don't know much about the Bible. But no, it is not a problem that people don't know much about the Bible.

I know this sounds like a contradiction, but it is not. Many pastors, preachers, and professors today say that the reason people don't live according to Scripture is because they don't know the Scriptures. If they only knew more about the Scriptures, so the argument goes, they would be more likely to live according to them. But again, decades (even centuries) of evidence proves that this is not how it works.

The real problem of today (and throughout all of history) is not getting people to know more about the Bible, but getting people to put into practice the parts of the Bible they already know. And no amount of preaching and teaching is going to fix this. The problem of people not living according to the Bible is not solved by filling their heads with more Bible facts and trivia.

What then is the solution? We must preach less, not more. Then, with the additional time that has been freed up by less teaching, church leaders can actually lead the church to practice what was preached. The pastor can lead the church to live and love like Jesus in the community and around the world. We can no longer believe the lie that it is enough to include specific points of application at the end of a carefully crafted sermon. Points of application no longer suffice. Leaders must actually lead the people into obedience. People don't want to (and shouldn't!) learn more about the Bible until they have seen the practical benefit in their lives and in the world of living out what they have already learned.

I once read a story of a monk who was reading Scripture one day when all of a sudden, he slammed the book shut, walked briskly out of the monastery with the Bible under his arm and took it to the nearest bookseller, where he sold it. On his way back to the monastery, he gave the money to a beggar on the street.

When he got back to the monastery, his fellow monks asked what he had read in Scripture which had offended him so much to cause him to sell his only Bible. "I was not offended," he told them. "I was obeying. I read where Jesus instructed a man to sell all he had and give it to the poor. So I obeyed."

I don't believe selling our Bibles is the answer. But I do want to suggest that before we attend another Bible study or listen to another sermon, we put into practice what we already know. I propose that before we learn more about the Bible, we obey that which we have already learned.

Yes, most Christians don't know much about the Bible, and this is a problem. But, the sad reality, is that most Christians also don't put into practice that which they already know, and this is an even greater problem. The solution is not to get them to learn more, but to live more. And the people need permission—even leadership!—from the pastors to get up out of the pews and into the community to put into practice what they already know.

I firmly believe that, despite the reports of vast biblical illiteracy among Christians today, we know enough of the Bible and what it teaches that it would take at least a year to put into practice what we already know. We don't need more sermons and studies. We just need to go out and start living the truth we have already learned. And until we have learned to live out what we know, we do not need to learn more.

Let me propose something radical. It may actually be that the biblical illiteracy reported in the studies and statistics—if true—is actually a *result* of God at work in our lives, rather than an indication of His absence. One clear scriptural principle is that God does not teach us more until we have learned to obey what we already know, and if we do not put into practice what we know, even what we know will be taken from us (see Luke 8:17-18). So it may be that the correction for widespread biblical illiteracy today is not more teaching, but more doing. (For an explanation of why biblical illiteracy is not a bad thing, see Appendix I.)

So what can a pastor do? How can we teach the Scriptures so that people not only learn what they say, but also do what is taught? The answer is not to teach more sermons, or to provide better and more concrete application. As we close out this chapter, let me propose two ways to teach the Bible, and (more importantly) teach the people to obey the Bible.

INTERACTIVE TEACHING

First, since this section of the book is about preaching, let me write a brief word about preaching and teaching. I propose that in order to make sure that our times of teaching and preaching are relevant to the needs and questions of the people who are seeking to follow Jesus into the world, we make our times of teaching as interactive as possible. I do not care if you are more of a topical teacher, or a book-by-book teacher, we must move away from the monologue model, and allow interaction from those we are teaching. Ideally, this may involve a complete reversal of the popular mindset in today's churches that the Sunday morning service is the most important church event of the week, and the midweek gatherings of smaller community groups are secondary.

Near the end of my years as a professional, paid pastor, as I was beginning to change some of my views and ideas about church and pastoral ministry, I started to try to impress upon the people of the church that if they could only attend one gathering of the church per week, I would prefer they go to a small group gathering rather than to the Sunday morning service. At this gathering, they could get better community, encouragement, accountability, and service opportunities than they ever could receive in a Sunday morning church service. If I were ever to return to pastoral ministry, I would emphasize this again. This is one good way of encouraging more interaction and dialogue.

But we can go further and do more to encourage dialogue and interaction. I know of several churches that have a mid-week "Pastor's Study" which is taught by the pastor and is devoted to reviewing the sermon that was preached the previous Sunday and answering any questions that people might have. This might be a good idea, except that it creates one more thing for people to attend and probably less than 5% of the congregation will show up for it. Furthermore, this study separates the actual interaction from the actual teaching by several days. By this time, questions and issues that may have been raised during the sermon are long forgotten.

I also know of churches that have set up online chat rooms, forums, and Facebook groups where people can interact with each other and with the pastor during the week about the sermon. Again, this is a move in the right direction, but it limits the interaction to those who have time to do it and it separates the interaction from the initial time of teaching.

A few churches have tried to overcome the time separation by providing a short Question and Answer session after every sermon. Sometimes this is in a side room after the service concludes, but very few people usually take advantage of this because it cuts into their lunch plans. To counter this, I know of some churches that offer a free meal or BBQ for people who want to stay afterward and discuss the message with the pastor. Everybody loves a free meal, and in the churches that I have seen do this, the turnout is often surprisingly large.

Occasionally, I have seen churches have an "open mic" time after the message, where a microphone is passed around to those who have questions. This practice is somewhat better, since the questions and answers benefit everyone who just heard the sermon, but often, only the bravest people will ask a question or make a comment. On the other hand, some people become very long-winded when they get a microphone in their hands and in a large-group setting it is difficult to keep their comment from turning into a second sermon. To counter this, I have seen a few churches have people turn in their questions and comments on slips of paper, and while this allows more interaction, it seemed less personal.

One intriguing way to encourage interaction during a sermon has only been recently enabled by the benefits of modern technology. I have seen some churches provide free WiFi to the congregation, and then invite people to bring their laptops, smartphones, and iPads to church so that they can text in questions via a messaging app or even on Twitter. Using such technology, people can make comments, ask questions, and generally interact with the sermon, sometimes while it is being preached. Though some might find this annoying, almost everyone today has developed the skill of listening to a message while reading small bits of information on a screen. The nightly news is the perfect example of this. You can listen to a news anchor run through the news of the day while at the same time read the scrolling news blurbs along the bottom of the screen. There is no reason people cannot do the same thing during a sermon.

But what about if we did away with most of the "audience"

focused times of teaching completely, and instead went to an online model where interaction is naturally built in, and where people are already doing a lot of their day-to-day learning? Earlier in this book I mentioned that the early church performed public proclamations of the good news about Jesus and the Kingdom of God, and then used times of detailed teaching to train and disciple believers. The reason the early church seemed to do this is because this is how the Roman Empire spread public proclamations and how popular teachers and philosophers spread their ideas to the masses.

So it would be wise to ask ourselves how information gets spread today. How does the government get the news out about new programs and benefits? How do companies spread word about their products and services? How to politicians win people over to vote for them and support their proposals? The three main avenues for all of these are television, radio, and the internet. So why not use these three avenues as our main way of teaching and reaching the Christians around us as well? Indeed, these three avenues are actually the way most Christians already get most of their information about the Bible. So why not consciously embrace it? If you want to reach people where they are at and teach people what they need to know, one of the easiest and simplest (and cheapest) things you can do is start a blog.

I myself started a blog about fifteen years ago for this very purpose, and I recently started a podcast to go with it. At the time of writing this (and I do not say any of this to boast), I have over 55,000 people read my blog posts every week. This is staggering to realize, especially when you know that Joel Osteen, who pastors the largest church in America, has about 45,000 people a week attend his church. Even though you may live in a town with less than 50 people, you can have a similar reach as Joel Osteen through the blessing of the internet. Jesus and the apostles used the teaching methods that were popular in their day to spread the good news about the Gospel and teach people how to live like Jesus. We can do the same today. Best of all, the internet is perfectly made for interactive teaching. In many ways, the internet is like a nonstop conversation between millions of people.

The bottom line is that there are numerous options for making your sermons and times of teaching more interactive. I have only suggested a few, but with some creativity and flexibility you may be able to come up with others. In this way, you will better be able to dialogue with the people who come to you for learning, and will also be able to provide better direction and guidance for how they can live out these truths in their lives. This, in fact, is the goal. To fully complete the learning cycle, we need to immediately put into practice what we have learned. Interactive teaching should always lead to interactive obeying.

INTERACTIVE OBEYING

For many sermons across the United States and around the world, the application section of a sermon consists of something close to the following words: "May the Lord apply to your lives what we have learned today. Let's pray." This is completely inadequate.

I understand that application is difficult to come up with, but if it is difficult for the pastor, it is doubly difficult for the person who has not been preparing the sermon all week. In a monologue message, the pastor must diligently strive to provide concrete and clear examples of how a message can be applied to the people who listen. Thankfully, more and more pastors understand this, so that some sermons I have heard recently are nearly 100% specific and concrete application. Yet I am not sure this is any better, since application without specific truth from Scripture is like skin on a body without bones. Application needs a foundation of Scriptural truth for structure, balance, and validity.

So what can the pastor do? Well, again, to some degree, this problem we face is due in part to the monologue nature of our messages. If the pastor is the one who does all the studying, preparing, and talking, then he is also the one who has to come up with the application. And even then, simply speaking application ideas provides no guarantee that people will actually follow through with the application. But if there is dialogue and interaction, then to some degree, the one leading the discussion can learn from and depend upon others in the community to come up with specific and concrete application of the truths that are learned. Then, once some of the ideas are developed, the "teacher" can actually lead the people out into the community to put these ideas into practice. In this way, we actually lead others to follow Jesus rather than just telling people how to do it on their own.

The great need in the church today is for pastors to start leading people into the community to put into practice the truths they have learned. If we really follow the example of Jesus, the teaching that is provided should never be separated from the ministry that is performed. The application of a sermon should involve inviting the people to an additional function later in the day or later in the week where they can see and follow the pastor as he puts into practice that which he taught. I call this "Putting service back into the church service." Most church services have very little actual service, but if pastors lead their church as suggested here, the church service actually becomes a service into the community.

More radical still, what if the teaching time did not take place during a 90-minute "service" on Sunday morning, but instead took place during a 9-minute bus ride down to feed the homeless, care for battered women, or pick up trash in the children's park? What if the teaching time was "on the way teaching" as the people drove to and from the place of ministry? Talk about tangible teaching!

Let's say a church was going to serve at a local woman's shelter that was ten minutes away. The people could gather at the church and take a bus to the shelter. On the way to the shelter, the pastor could lay the biblical groundwork for why we take care of orphans and widows, and provide some special tips for dealing with battered women. Then the church could serve at the shelter for an hour or two, and on the way home, the pastor could address any issues or questions that had arisen. Altogether, this would take about two or three hours, and would function as the actual church service for the week. It could even take place on Sunday morning so that there is not "one more thing" for the people to cram into their busy schedules.

If hundreds or thousands of people are involved, and they cannot all fit into a bus, the pastor could train "bus teachers" in advance on what to say, or use some other similar method of discipleship. In general, the goal is to immediately put into practice what is learned, and then immediately address any needs or issues that arose as a result of what was done. This is true biblical teaching, and would lead to true Christlike living.

Even smaller churches or house churches can incorporate

more community services into their main meetings and teaching times of the week. If 10 or 20 people are meeting in a living room for prayer and discussion, they can easily take those discussions on the road and find a place in the community to serve as part of their weekly community activity.

Listen to these decisive words from Jacques Ellul:

> When we have really understood the actual plight of our contemporaries, when we have heard their cry of anguish, and when we have understood why they won't have anything to do with our disembodied gospel, when we have shared their sufferings, both physical and spiritual, in their despair and desolation, when we have become one with the people of our own nation and of the universal church, as Moses and Jeremiah were one with their own people, as Jesus identified himself with the wandering crowds, "sheep without a shepherd," *then* we will be able to proclaim the Word of God—but not till then!
>
> To proclaim the word of God to men in the abstract, to people who are in a situation which prevents them from understanding it, means that we are tempting God. ...The church, which has received the "pearls" of the gospel, throws them with pious indifference as food to the "swine," who are human beings ... And these people turn against the church, saying, "We find no nourishment in your pearls, no satisfaction in their beauty. What are we to do with them? They are no good to us in our present situation!" (And this is true!)[3]

Ultimately, teaching and preaching must no longer be simply

---

[3] Jacques Ellul, *The Presence of the Kingdom* (Colorado Springs: Helmers & Howard, 1989), 116-117.

a time where one person gets up and delivers a lecture about some topic or Bible passage, only for the people to go home until they do it all again next week. This accomplishes nothing for the Kingdom of God and nothing for the world we are to serve. We must get out of the pews, step down from the pulpit, and learn Scripture together by discussing what it says with one another and then putting into practice in our communities what we have learned. It is only in this way that the Word of God ignites like fire within our hearts and minds and creates change both in our lives and in our communities. Once we stop preaching, we can then start living. In this way, the light of the Gospel will rise in our lives and people will know that Jesus truly is within us.

DISCUSSION QUESTIONS

1. What are some possible reasons for canceling the Sunday sermon?

2. What is the ultimate goal of learning the Scriptures?

3. What is "on the way teaching"?

4. What is the main reason so few Christians actually practice the words and teachings of Jesus?

5. Rather than biblical illiteracy, what is the *real* problem with the modern church?

6. What is a practical thing pastors can do to teach people about how to follow Jesus?

7. Provide some examples of interactive and "on the way" teaching that might work in your community.

8. Ultimately, what is the main goal of preaching and teaching, and how can a pastor best accomplish this goal with the people in the church?

PART III: DISCARD THE DOCTRINAL STATEMENT

The world has yet to see what God will do through a worldwide church whose members love one another.
—*N. T. Wright*

Christianity has become a religion of words. Although following Jesus should lead to a life of action, much of Christianity spends a lot of time arguing about words, and especially some of the words found in the so-called "Word of God," the Bible. Yet the Bible, when properly read and understood, points us to one Word, the true Word, which is Jesus Christ. To state this another way, the Bible, a book of words from God, points us to Jesus, the Word of God. In my book, *How Can I Study the Bible?* I state that the Bible is the *written* Word of God which teaches us to follow Jesus, the *living* Word of God.

Yet there is a problem. We have divorced the written Word of God from the living Word of God. As followers of Jesus, we are to live like Jesus and love others like Jesus, but far too often, Christianity degenerates into arguing about words related to Jesus, rather than living like Jesus. Rather than love for the Word leading us to love the world, our focus on arguing about words has created war over words that has swept through Christianity and destroyed our witness in the world.

Saddest of all is that as a result of our war of words, Christians not only fail to love others, but actually go and kill others instead. Beginning in the fourth century AD, continuing all the way through the Middle Ages and the Reformation, and even up into modern days, it is not uncommon to hear about one group of Christians seeking to slander, destroy, imprison, and even kill other Christians with whom they disagree theologically. About the only time Christians seem to agree with each other is when we unite together to slander, destroy, and kill other groups in Jesus' name.[1]

For the first 350 years of church history, Christians were persecuted by others. But once Christianity became the official religion of the Roman Empire and gained all the power inherent within that position, the persecuted quickly became the persecutors. We hunted down and killed not only those who refused to convert to Christianity, but also those Christians who held to different theological beliefs than those of the church leaders.

Sadly, these heretic hunts were usually caused by a disagreement over some theological word or definition. Indeed, sometimes the arguments were over a single letter. For example, one of the major theological debates in the fourth and fifth century AD concerned the Greek words *homoousion* and *homoiousion*. Do you

---

[1] See J. D. Myers, *Nothing but the Blood of Jesus* (Dallas, OR: Redeeming Press, 2017) for why this happens and what we can do about it.

see the extra *iota* (*i*) in the middle of that second word? While the first word means "same" the second word means "similar." The debate over these words concerned the nature of Jesus Christ. The question was this: Was Jesus the *same* as God or just *similar* to God? If He was fully God, then in what way was He human? Was He one person, or two? How did His divinity and humanity interact? Though the theological scuffle waged for many years, the church eventually decided in 451 AD that Jesus had two natures in one person.

Many Christians did not agree with this decision, and in 457 "Jerusalem was occupied by an army of monks [where] in the name of the one incarnate nature, they pillaged, they burnt, they murdered; the Sepulcher of Christ was defiled with blood."[2] Then on the third day before Easter, the mob entered the baptistery of a city church and butchered the Bishop Dioscorus, along with six other clergy members, then paraded the bleeding corpses around the city, before burning the remains and scattering the ashes to the wind.

Do not misunderstand. The issue of whether or not Jesus is fully God is an important question. But regardless of how important the issue is, if debates and arguments about this issue lead one group to kill and murder their theological opponents, I think they have completely misunderstood the "Jesus" they are arguing about. Jesus would rather people believe something wrong about Him than to have people kill others in His name because they want to add a single *iota* to a word.

---

[2] Diarmaid MacCulloch, *Christianity: The First 3000 Years* (New York: Penguin, 2011), 441.

Yet such violence over theology is not an isolated incident in Christianity. This violent trend over words continued throughout church history. For example, some members of Eastern Orthodoxy cut out the tongue and amputated the right hand of a teacher named Maximus for teaching that Jesus Christ participated in fully human activity and had a fully human will.[3] They believed that without a tongue to speak or a hand to write, he would no longer be able to teach what they had condemned as "heresy."

During the Crusades, there was the widespread slaughter of the Albegensians, who held to a dualistic rejection of all things material in order to achieve spiritual purity.

In the days of the Reformation, John Calvin burned Servetus at the stake for denying the Trinity. But he was not alone in this. Zwingli had several Anabaptists drowned for their belief in getting rebaptized as adults. After Martin Luther wrote a document defending that all people were equal under God, thousands of German peasants rose up in revolt against the German lords. Luther saw this as an even greater sin, and so he wrote that the "murdering, thieving hordes of the peasants" … "must be knocked to pieces, strangled and stabbed, covertly and overtly, by everyone who can, just as one must kill a mad dog." The German lords sent their armies out to do this very thing, and thousands were killed.

Though such theological murders are not as common today, they still take place in various parts of the world. Although, in general, the issues today are not as much over theological disa-

---

[3] See, for example, J. R. Mantey, "Evidence that the Perfect Tense in John 20:23 and Matthew 16:19 is Mistranslated," *JETS* 19 (Summer, 1973).

greements as they are with economic and social disagreements. Theology is just used as an excuse. Even then, Christians today rarely murder others in the name of Jesus. Instead, we attempt to slander, abuse, and even destroy the jobs or incomes of other Christians who have different social or political views than our own.

When some Christians discover that certain other Christians have different beliefs or theological ideas, they may refuse to do business with them, shun them in public places, and often speak negatively about them to others. Occasionally, nasty letters (or even books) of condemnation will be written. Worse yet, some people seek to get others fired from their jobs. It is not uncommon for pastors, professors, and other church leaders to call for the termination of other pastors, professors, and church leaders over a book that was published, a sermon that was preached, or a lecture that was taught, in which some questionable theological statements were made.

I myself was terminated from a job in a Christian non-profit organization because I was investigating and reading some doctrines and theological ideas which made the President of the organization nervous. Though my job performance was faultless and not a single one of the doctrines I was studying had anything to do with the doctrinal statement of the organization, the President thought that if donors heard that I was studying these doctrines, support for the organization would decrease. So he fired me.

As a result of my termination, all of my Christians friends abandoned me. They thought that I must have sinned in some way to be terminated from my job at a Christian organization. I received dozens of emails from friends and family explaining that they were going to separate themselves from me until I repented of my sin. Only then could I be restored to fellowship with them. When I explained that I had not sinned, but had only been investigating alternative theological views, they did not believe me and claimed that I was becoming hard-of-heart in my unrepentance.

After this, I was black-balled in the Christian community. Nobody wanted to hire me at their church or organization, because none of my former Christian friends and acquaintances felt they could give me a positive character reference. Though I had just earned a Master's of Theology degree from a leading seminary, the degree was worthless because I had been shunned by other Christians.

It took me nearly three months to find a new job. Though I applied for over 100 jobs, the only job I could find was as a carpet cleaner. I worked 16-hour days at $100 per day. I racked up a lot of debt, my marriage suffered, and my health declined (I ended up needing two surgeries as a result of that job). Finally, ten months after getting fired from the non-profit organization, I found another one that provided more of a long-term solution for my family's needs.

For many years afterward, I struggled with severe depression. On the day I was fired, my entire life was swept away. All of my hopes, dreams, plans, training, education, experience, and friends disappeared. I was left with nothing. I felt that everything had been stripped away from me, that I had nothing to look forward to in life, and that each day I woke up was worse than the one before. It was a very dark time in my life, when I needed other Christians around me most. But because I read some "taboo" books, I had been completely shunned.

I don't share this to garner pity or support, or even to blame the President of that organization. I still believe in what that organization is doing, and agree with their mission and theology. I only share my story to point out that while we may not kill others today over theological issues, we do destroy the lives of others when we seek to end their jobs or careers because they took a theological path that make us uncomfortable. Since that time, I have talked with dozens of pastors and former church leaders who have experienced similar treatment from churches and church leaders in which they used to serve. So though we no longer kill, we still seek to hurt, damage, and destroy—all in the name of "correct theology," all in the name of words.

In light of this failure to follow Jesus as the Word because of arguments over words, the following chapters of this book continue the theme begun previously. In previous chapters, we looked at how Christianity piles up preachers who give us what our itching ears want to hear until we are so intent on learning more about Scripture that we fail to obey the truth we already know. In this part of the book, we see another area where excessive words have created a substitute—and even a barrier—to love. This area is that of church doctrinal statements. In the following two chapters, I argue that the church should discard their doctrinal statements.

Please note carefully what I am and am *not* saying. When I urge the church to give up doctrinal statements, I am not saying we should give up doctrine. Nor am I saying that we should try to find the bare minimum of doctrine on which all agree and then believe and teach only that. A watered-down Christianity is not worth believing. It is important to ask the hard questions. We should not tolerate the idea that certain ideas cannot be tolerated. It is critical to study long and hard. It is vital that we dot our doctrinal i's and cross our theological t's. It is essential for razor-sharp minds to delve deep into the quandaries and questions of Scripture and theology.

But, as we continue to study, think, and learn, it is vitally important that we never use the tentative results of our studies (all theology is tentative, for there is never any such thing as a final conclusion to theology) to bring damage, division, and disunity to the people of God. When doctrine leads to division in this way, it is being misused and abused. The following two chapters show why this happens and how we can avoid it. This part of the book is about the good, the bad, and the ugly aspects of doctrinal statements. Let us consider the bad and the ugly first.

CHAPTER 7

BAD AND UGLY DOCTRINAL STATEMENTS

It is historically uncertain when, where, and how the first doctrinal statements were developed. It is likely that some of the first creeds are found in Scripture, in passages like Philippians 2:5-11, 1 Corinthians 15:3-6, and 1 Timothy 3:16. However, some believe that these were not exactly creeds, but hymns. Furthermore, these Scriptural statements are not exactly creedal confession of doctrine, but are summaries of stories about Jesus. They are narrative summaries; not doctrinal summaries.

Some also point to the statement that came out of the Jerusalem council in Acts 15:23-29 as an early statement of belief. Yet Acts 15 does not contain a doctrinal statement. The letter from the church leaders in Acts 15 is not a statement of belief, but a statement of behaviors. It is not telling Gentile Christians what they must believe, but rather, telling them what they must do.

These two ideas, that the early statements were based primarily on the narrative of Scripture and the behavior of believers, will become critical later in this book for understanding how we, as twenty-first century followers of Jesus, can stand up for truth without needing the damaging and destructive doctrinal statements that have divided Christianity for so long. For now, let us continue to see how doctrinal statements began to develop.

Once we get past the era of the New Testament church, two early statements were developed, the Nicene Creed and the Apostles' Creed. Some believe that the Nicene Creed was first, but I believe that it was preceded by the Apostles' Creed, even though the Apostles were probably not the ones who wrote it.

The Apostles' Creed says this:

> I believe in God the Father Almighty,
> Maker of heaven and earth:
> And in Jesus Christ His only Son our Lord,
> Who was conceived by the Holy Ghost,
> Born of the Virgin Mary,
> Suffered under Pontius Pilate,
> Was crucified, dead, and buried:
> He descended into hell;
> The third day He rose again from the dead;
> He ascended into heaven,
> And sitteth on the right hand of God the Father Almighty;
> From thence he shall come to judge the living and the dead.
> I believe in the Holy Ghost;
> The holy Catholic Church;
> The communion of Saints;
> The forgiveness of sins;
> The resurrection of the body,
> And the life everlasting.
> Amen.

This is a good doctrinal statement. And if this had been the only doctrinal statement ever developed, I would not be writing this chapter. The Apostle's Creed is simple, concise, and comprehensive. It contains most of the basic beliefs of Christianity, and there is nothing in there that the majority of Christians throughout history would disagree with.

Yet the simplicity of the Apostles' Creed is also its flaw. The statement is not as precise as we would like about many things that are considered "essential beliefs" by many Christians. For example, though the Father, Son, and Holy Spirit are mentioned, the statement does not talk about their Trinitarian relationship. Furthermore, the statement is ambiguous about the full divinity and humanity of Jesus, or His sinlessness and pre-existence. And while it does mention belief in the Holy Spirit, the church, the forgiveness of sin, the resurrection of the body, and life everlasting, it doesn't say *what* the church believes about these things, such as how they are obtained, what they look like, or how they function. Finally, the statement says absolutely nothing about the Bible.

The real issue, however, is not really what the Apostle's Creed says, but why it was written. If God has given us Scripture, why do we need doctrinal statements? The various answers are numerous and complex, but ultimately, it comes down to one main thing. The church began to develop doctrinal statements in order to know who is "in" and who is "out." Throughout history, people disagree on what Scripture actually teaches, and so doctrinal statements were written to serve as a guide for the proper interpretation and understanding of Scripture.

Honestly, this sounds like a good idea as it seems that the goal was to create unity within the Body of Christ. The problem, however, is that the opposite happened. Instead of bringing about unity and love, doctrinal statements created division and strife. People began to use doctrinal statements as a way of deciding who was a true believer and who was not. They used creeds to determine who belonged to the church and who did not. So although unity was the goal of doctrinal statements, division was the actual result.

From the simplicity of this Apostles' Creed spawned an ever-increasing number of doctrinal statements, with ever-increasing length and complexity. Some of the more well-known and famous doctrinal statements of church history include the following:

- The Nicene Creed (325 AD)
- The Second Nicene Creed (381 AD)
- The Definition of Chalcedon (451 AD)
- The Canons of Constantinople (869 AD)
- The Augsburg Confession (1530 AD)
- The First Helvitic Confession (1536 AD)
- The Council of Trent (1542-1563 AD)
- The Belgic Confession (1561 AD)
- The Thirty-Nine Article (1571 AD)
- The Canons of Dordt (1618 AD)
- The Westminster Confession (1646 AD)
- Vatican II (1962-1965 AD)
- The Chicago Statement on Inerrancy (1978 AD)

These are only some of the more well-known and widely accepted doctrinal statements. Today, there are thousands of different doctrinal statements for the thousands of different denominations, churches, and ministries. While the vast majority of these doctrinal statements were created primarily for the purpose of defining one group's distinctive beliefs without condemning those who believe differently, nearly every one of these statements contains points that are considered "non-negotiable" and which cause churches and Christians to separate from others who believe differently. Many of these doctrinal statements even cause those who follow it to condemn those who hold to other beliefs as "unsaved."

Ultimately, the reason behind the development of all these statements remains the same. While on the surface, people claim that the statements help Christians know the truth, the statements ultimately create an atmosphere which allows us to control and condemn others. If you think that this is not what happens with doctrinal statements, try suggesting to the pastor of your church that you do not agree with some of the points in the doctrinal statement and that the church should change or discard it. He will most often say something like this:

> We need the doctrinal statement so people know what we believe, and so we can take a stand on the truth. If we were to get rid of it, how would we know who could teach Sunday school, who could lead Bible studies, and who could preach sermons? What is stopping a Mormon, or a Jehovah's Witness, or a Universalist, or an Arminian from becoming a member and teaching their heresy to others?

Do you see? People want to know who is a true Christian and who is not. They want to be able to divide the saints from the sinners, the Orthodox from the Heretics. They want to know who is in and who is out. And doctrinal statements help them do this.

Again, taking a stand for truth is always commendable. Those who write doctrinal statements are hoping to define and defend the truth, to protect it from all the lies and false teaching that is out there. The Bible is full of instructions to stand for what is right and true, and as followers of Jesus, who is Truth, we must stand up for truth.

It just does not seem that the development of doctrinal statements has helped protect the truth in the way we hoped they would. There are three ways we use doctrinal statements to destroy. First, we use them to set ourselves up as judge in place of Jesus. This becomes even more grievous when we disagree with the judgments of Jesus and end up judging Jesus Himself! Second, we use the creeds to kill the truth and destroy people rather than defend the truth or protect people. Finally, we use the creeds to gut the gospel and ignore the entire point of the teachings of Jesus. Let us look at each of these three problems below.

JUDGING JESUS

The first major problem with the way doctrinal statements are used is that they tend to set up individual churches and church leaders as judges over the eternal destiny of others, rather than leave this up to Jesus. Yes, the church is supposed to judge others, but only in areas of personal disagreements and breaking the law (1 Cor 5:12; 6:1-6), not in the areas of eternal destiny. Far too often, doctrinal statements are used to issue anathemas against other groups who believe different doctrines, or to issue excommunications from the church and consign others to the pit of hell for all eternity.

Nowhere in Scripture, however, do we read that churches or individual Christians are supposed to make such determinations. Jesus alone is the judge of others in regard to their eternal destiny. When we tell people that they are going to hell because they read the Bible differently than we do or believe something we think is incorrect, we have usurped the role of Jesus. Yes, we can disagree with others. Yes, we can tell others that we think they are wrong. Yes, we can debate and discuss doctrine. But we can never tell others that because they disagree with us, they will spend eternity in hell. It is not our place to say such things or make such judgments.

We make these judgments of others for two reasons, one that is public and one that is private. We *say* we make judgments about the eternal destiny of others because we have concern for them and where they will spend eternity. And this is a legitimate concern. No Christian wants any person to spend eternity separated from God. But privately, the reason we judge and condemn others is because we fear that we ourselves might be wrong. Since no person is 100% correct in everything, we know that we all have wrong beliefs. Yet since it is difficult to figure out where our wrong beliefs are or face the fact that we might be wrong, one psychological defense we use is to condemn those who believe differently.

This fear of our own wrong beliefs causes us to try to force others to believe as we do. If we can get them to believe what we believe, then this affirms that our beliefs are correct. And the simplest way to get others to agree is to make them afraid of disagreeing. We say, "If you don't believe like I do, you are going to hell." Of course, while this works on some people, others simply respond with the same argument thrown right back: "No. I'm not the one going to hell; you are—unless you change your beliefs to match mine."

In such a situation, we are at a theological impasse. If I say you are headed to hell because you don't believe the way I do, and you say the same thing back at me, how are we to decide who is right and who is wrong? The historical solution is that both sides make a doctrinal statement and then get as many people as possible to agree with it. The side with the most votes wins.

For example, some suggest that the primary reason Emperor Constantine called for the Council of Nicaea in 325 AD was so that he could attempt to create peace between the escalating rhetoric between those who supported Athanasius (who argued for the eternal divinity of Jesus) and Arius (who argued that Jesus was not eternally divine). Constantine did not want to see his fledgling Christian Empire collapse as a result of a theological dispute, and so he invited all 1800 church bishops to attend.

About 300 bishops arrived for the council, and while the vast majority of these supported the view of Athanasius (some suggest that the Bishops who supported the views of Arius were threatened to stay away), they still had trouble developing a doctrinal statement that all present could accept. Finally, Emperor Constantine suggested the addition of the word *homoousius* (of one essence, or the same) be added to the statement as a way of describing the nature of Jesus in connection to the nature of God. The Emperor also declared that anyone who disagreed with the statement would be excommunicated from the church and exiled from the Empire. Not surprisingly, there were only two votes of dissent among the gathered bishops.

In church history, however, some groups were not content with voting, and instead sought to protect their position and increase their influence through violence. Doctrinal differences have occasionally led to wars between factions as each side tries to exert power and control over others. As we will see in the next section, creeds can kill. But on a smaller scale, and this is what we often see today, individual pastors or church leaders try to maintain their own power and prominence by stifling all dissent or disagreement with threats of church discipline, loss of membership, excommunication, or even eternal condemnation.

Sadly, these actions often have less to do with doctrine, and more to do with consolidating power, authority, and popularity. Sometimes a doctrinal statement is developed simply to maintain control and get rid of those who disagree. The statement allows leaders to determine who is "in" and who is "out," who can teach and who must remain silent. Doctrinal statements place people in the position of judge over others.

In these cases, doctrinal statements are not about truth at all, but are instead about control. Doctrinal statements do not lead to greater love and service, but to manipulation and condemnation. They are more about domination than discipleship. They help a ruling class stay in power, silencing all dissent with the threat of both temporal and eternal punishment. But again, determining someone's eternal destiny is not a function of individual Christians, or of the church in general, but is a task for Jesus alone. You and I do not determine people's eternal destiny: only He does. When we use doctrinal statements to judge others, we are saying that we cannot wait for Jesus to do His job at the Great White Throne Judgment, and we want it done now; that we cannot wait to hear what Jesus has to say so we must do His job for Him.

In such a way, we are not only telling Jesus that His timing is not right, we are also saying His decisions cannot be trusted. When we take over the role of determining the eternal destiny of others, we are not only judging them, we are also judging Jesus. I don't know about you, but this is not something I want to be part of. Far too often, when the decisions of the church disagree with the decisions of Jesus, we end up finding creative ways to explain away the judgments of Jesus and set our own up as the good and lawful decrees. But if we are disagreeing with Jesus, then our degrees are not good and lawful, but are more likely to be sinful and satanic. When this happens, the creeds no longer bring life, but are used to kill, steal, and destroy.

CREEDS KILL

Jesus once said while the thief comes to steal, kill, and destroy, He came that we might have life, and have it to the full (John 10:10). If we use the creeds of Christendom to give anything but life, liberty, and freedom, then we are not using them to accomplish the will of Jesus, but to work with the thief in destroying the lives of others.

One of the most terrible uses of the creeds is when we use them to condemn others to hell, or worse yet, hasten them on their way to hell. Indeed, killing others so they go to hell often follows upon the heels of condemning to hell. When we use doctrinal statements to determine the eternal destiny of other people—which is something only Jesus should do—it is not long before we get the idea that if a person is a reprobate heretic, it is better to send them on their way to hell than to let them stick around and lead others astray.

Such thinking was actually evident in the apostles of Jesus before the church even began. At one point in the ministry of Jesus, the people of a Samaritan village rejected Jesus. The disciples became incensed that the village had turned them away, so two of the disciples, James and John, asked Jesus if they could call down fire from heaven to consume and destroy the town and everybody in it (Luke 9:54). They figured that people who didn't act like them, look like them, and believe like them, were under the curse of God and were fit only to be destroyed.

The response of Jesus is telling. Not only does He *not* give them permission to call down fire from heaven, but He goes further and rebukes such an attitude. He says, "You do not know what manner of spirit you are of! For the Son of Man did not come to destroy men's lives but to save them" (Luke 9:55-56).

Burning people for rejecting Jesus does not reflect the heart or mission of Jesus. I am sure we can extrapolate this out and also say that calling people stupid, dumb, foolish, or ignorant for believing something different also does not reflect the heart of Jesus for all people. Nor does trying to ruin their lives, get them fired from their jobs, destroy their incomes, or pray for their demise. To repeat the words of Jesus, those who act this way do not know what manner of spirit they are of.

Yet such a spirit of hatred and destruction of others has been the *modus operandi* for the church since almost day one.

Very early in the life of the church, creeds and doctrinal statements became tools in the hands of political and religious leaders to control crowds and dominate others. While taxation and imprisonment is often a good way to force others to support your cause and obey your laws, such tools do not always work among those who serve a Higher Power or believe they are following a Divine Law which supersedes human courts. "We must serve God rather than men" is a concept found within all religions.

So when Christianity became the state religion of the Roman

Empire in the fourth century AD, church and political rulers joined forces to accomplish God's will "on earth, as it is in heaven." They saw great benefit in being able to decide where a person would spend eternity, based on how they believed and behaved. There is great power in showing that God and the state are in agreement on an issue, for then you can call on the masses to serve God *by* serving men.

Of course, even among the church leadership, not everybody believed the same thing. Disagreements arose among them about what the Bible actually taught, until eventually, both sides condemned and excommunicated their opponents. This led to heated theological debates, and even military skirmishes and minor wars. In an attempt to keep the peace, councils were called and creeds were formed to help determine which side was correct. Roman Emperors often became involved in these debates, and occasionally it was an Emperor who made the final decision about which theological perspective was correct.

These doctrinal disputes were not so much determined by who had the majority, but by who had the most power and influence in the Roman Empire. This was especially true when one side could gain the support of the Emperor. Whichever side had the ear of the Emperor were most likely to win the debate. And how does one get the ear of the Emperor? Usually, something more is needed than logical arguments about biblical passages. Rulers tend to care more about their coffers and their borders than what the Bible says. Therefore, money, power, and land were often used to gain the support of the Emperor and other authorities, rather than sound reasoning from the Bible.

Once the Emperor made his decision about a theological issue, the losing side was often condemned, not only to eternal punishment in hell, but sometimes even to death by stoning, beheading, hanging, or by what became the most popular method: burning at the stake. Emperors do not like it when people in their Empire disagree with them. Dissent was seen as a threat to the peace, order, and prosperity of the Empire. The simplest way to gain unity within the Empire was to get rid of dissenters by killing them.

Though most Christians do not want to admit it today, this was the process by which much of our traditional theology was developed. It was not through careful exegesis and logical debate of what the Scriptures say, but through power politics, greedy rulers, and declaring war on all who disagreed.[1]

How do we explain this horrendous behavior of past Christians?

The most popular way is to say that Christians of the past were influenced by their culture, and so were not at fault. Just take one famous and contested example: the execution of Servetus by being burned at the stake. The primary accusation against Servetus was that he denied infant baptism and the classical conception of the Trinity. There are numerous historical details surrounding his arrest, trial, and execution, but the main point is how modern Reformed historians explain these events. Here is one popular explanation from a well-known author:

The main facts therefore may now be summarized thus:

---

[1] For more on this, see Philip Jenkins, *Jesus Wars* (New York: HarperOne, 2010), and Greg Boyd, *The Myth of a Christian Nation* (Grand Rapids: Zondervan: 2005), chapters 4, 9.

1. That Servetus was guilty of blasphemy, of a kind and degree which is still punishable here in England by imprisonment.
2. That his sentence was in accordance with the spirit of the age.
3. That he had been sentenced to the same punishment by the Inquisition at Vienne.
4. That the sentence was pronounced by the Councils of Geneva, Calvin having no power either to condemn or to save him.
5. That Calvin and others visited the unhappy man in his last hours, treated him with much kindness, and did all they could to have the sentence mitigated.[2]

Having read many of the details about this trial and execution, here is how these five points could be worded differently:

1. Servetus did not believe in the Trinity or that babies should be baptized.
2. At that time, people killed others for such theological differences.
3. The Catholics did it too!
4. Calvin wrote a letter recommending that Servetus be killed, and the Council decided that Servetus "be burned alive, at a slow fire, till his body be reduced to a cinder."

---

[2] William Wileman, "Calvin and Servetus." https://bannerof truth.org/us/resources/articles/2003/calvin-and-servetus/

5. Calvin pleaded with Servetus to recant his views, and thus avoid death, but Servetus refused. Calvin requested that Servetus be beheaded rather than being burned at the stake, but his request was denied.

I am not trying to condemn Calvinism, the Genevan Council, or even John Calvin himself for such behavior. I am just saying that as Christians, we need to own up to our bloody past, and admit the truth: Yes, Christians have done some wicked, evil things in the name of Jesus and for the cause of proper theology. We should not try to explain these away. Doing so only makes us look foolish and like we are trying to hide something.

Honestly, trying to hide the skeletons in the historical Christian closet makes people wonder what we are trying to hide today as well. If we try to explain away and excuse Christian wars and crusades, investigations and inquisitions, or burnings and beheadings, it makes people wonder what we are trying to explain away today.

But we don't kill people for Christ today, do we? We don't go to war with those who disagree, right? We don't behead and burn people who voice dissent ... or do we? Maybe we have just become so good at explaining things away, that we still do all of these things today but just do not see it.

Even though we modern, civilized Christians typically do not kill and murder those with whom we disagree, there is an area of our lives today where we still put others to death for the sake of our religion. We still do kill others over theology.

I am thinking more about the Jihad that Christians have declared upon Muslims.

I can hear it now: "No, No! It is they who have declared Jihad upon America!"

Yes, but Jihad means "Holy War." It is a war which has a just and righteous cause. It is a war that God not only tells you to fight, but also fights with you on your side. And many Christians do believe these things about American wars. We don't call it Jihad; we call it a "Just War," a war with a righteous cause, a war in which God fights on our side. There is not much difference between "Jihad" and "Just War."

Do we really imagine that God goes out with us to kill other people? Do we really imagine that He helps our bullets fly accurately, and our bombs drop in the right spot to bring a bloody end to the lives of others?

To ask the question is to answer it.

Do not misunderstand. I'm not a pacifist. I *do* think that national leaders have the responsibility to defend and protect the nation and its citizens against threats. I believe that the leaders of every country should do what is necessary to protect their citizens against the sort of thing that happened on 9-11.

What I am opposed to, however, is how the politicians of our country so easily gained the support of the vast majority of Christian churches for war. Many churches thirsted for the blood of Saddam Hussein, Osama bin Laden, and the nameless mass of terrorists. When the churches got involved, what began as a "War on Terror" quickly became a "War on Muslim Extremists," and has now pretty much degenerated into a "War on Islam."

Church billboards went from signs that said, "God Bless America," to "God Bless our Troops," to things like "God will judge our enemies, but we'll arrange the meeting." I don't think that God rejoiced when Saddam or Osama died. Do I think that these men were upright, outstanding citizens of the world? Of course not. I just think that followers of Jesus should not be calling for the death of anyone, nor rejoicing when they die.

It is the right of nations and governments to go to war and execute criminals, but Christians should always be pleading and seeking for a middle ground between Pacifism and Just War.

Churches should not sit back and let the criminals of the world (or our own country) walk all over us, our families, and our freedoms, but nor should we teach that the killing and murder of others is the best way out. We must remind the world that there is nothing holy about a Holy War; there is nothing just in a Just War. And no matter what, we must not allow our theology to be used as a tool to justify the killing of other people.

But it is not just killing that we Christians justify in the name of God and sound theology. Though we sometimes kill with bombs and bullets in the name of "Just War," most of our "killing" is much less violent. We use creeds not only to kill, but also to ruin the lives of people by getting them fired from their jobs, or by destroying their families and finances by things we say, letters we write, and gossip we spread. These are ways that creeds kill.

Aside from the damage that creeds do to other people, they also cause great harm to the church. Creeds often destroy church creativity and unity. By seeking unity at all costs, we kill the creativity and liberty of others by forcing them to conform to our approved creeds and conduct. When we have an agreed-upon set of beliefs and behaviors, it is unacceptable for people to move beyond the boundaries of either one. Such limitations can stifle the Spirit-inspired creativity of God's people.

Some of the best exegetical and theological work that has ever been done in the history of the church was done in the early centuries before there were all the creeds and confessions to rein people in. Origen, for example, may have been one of the most creative Bible scholars the church has ever seen, and he came up with some great interpretations of Biblical texts. But he also came up with outlandish ideas, which were later condemned as heresy by the church. As a result, people barely study Origen today, because they are afraid of being outcast for reading and studying a "heretic."

Similarly today, pastors and professors who develop a fresh way of understanding a biblical text are often afraid to share it with others due to the theological backlash they are sure to receive. Seminaries and churches are filled with theological landmines that threaten to destroy the person who dares to tread outside the well-beaten path of traditional teaching. It's the same for Bible College and Seminary students. If such students want to graduate, they are discouraged from researching in new directions or challenging the *status quo* in the understanding of some biblical texts. The doctrinal statement of the school restrains and restricts any desire to learn, study, and think for themselves, and so all creative thinking is stifled. Creeds not only kill people, they also kill creativity.

Most ironically of all, creeds also kill church unity. Unity, according to Jesus, is one of the key ways that the church is to be recognized (John 13:35; 17:21). In other words, the church cannot properly function without unity. Yet while creeds and confessions were intended to bring people together over core elements of the faith, what actually happens is that doctrinal statements separates one group within the Body of Christ from another. The doctrinal differences are usually not that large, but they are significant enough to bring division and strife within the church.

BAD AND UGLY DOCTRINAL STATEMENTS 159

I think it saddens Jesus when there are dozens of groups of believers within the same town who are separated by a minor point of theology and so cannot love and serve others in the community as a unified group. When arguments about when Jesus will return or whether or not people can speak in tongues keep us from working together for the gospel, our creeds have killed the church.

> In spite of the fact that the original Reformers—particularly Luther—began the movement with a liberating rediscovery of free grace and dying love, their successors ... rapidly obscured that liberty by scholasticizing the stuffing out of it. Every church of the Reformation era (the Roman Church not excepted) fell in love with the idea of confecting long-winded confessions of faith—binding documents that spelled out in mind-numbing detail the correct positions to be held on all points at issue.[3]

The new ideas of the Reformation which initially reinvigorated the church, soon killed the church when people tried to codify, define, and defend all the new ideas with ever-lengthening doctrinal statements. In the end, the problem was just as bad as before: the creeds and confessions of the church caused us to completely miss the entire point of the gospel and the teaching of Jesus.

GUTTING THE GOSPEL

One of the greatest problems with doctrinal statements is what

---

[3] Robert Farrar Capon, *The Astonished Heart* (Grand Rapids: Eerdmans, 1996), 6.

they do to the gospel. While we believe that creeds and confessions protect the gospel, defending it against heresy, keeping at bay those who teach a false gospel, and leading people toward central truths of gospel—such as God's holiness, our sinfulness, and the person and work of Jesus Christ—they tend to do exactly the opposite. This is because the gospel is significantly more than a set of theological propositions.

If the gospel was nothing more than a set of propositions to believe, or a series of doctrines to defend, then creeds and confessions do a good job protecting the gospel. The problem is that while the gospel does contain doctrine, the gospel is not primarily about doctrine. The gospel is not simply about what we must believe. The gospel is much more than a set of Christian ideas.

When understood from Scripture, the gospel is closer to a way of life than a set of ideas.[4] Yes, the gospel contains ideas, but the *real* good news in the gospel is that the ideas of the gospel will lead to a whole new way of living, thinking, and acting. The gospel contains a new worldview which changes how we think about others and how we live life. The gospel not only contains ideas on what to believe, but also instructions on how to behave.

The gospel is about loving others like Jesus. It is about showing others what Jesus looks and acts like through our own life and actions. It is about living here on earth according to the rules of heaven. It is about freedom from trying to live up to the standards of men, and instead showing to the whole world a new way of life and liberty in Jesus Christ. The gospel helps people know

---

[4] See my online theology course, "The Gospel According to Scripture" for more. https://redeeminggod.com/courses/

peace, feel loved, experience contentment, and gain purpose. These are the exciting and invigorating elements of the gospel, and it is these that you will never find in any doctrinal statement. Without these life-transforming truths, the gospel is nothing but a lifeless set of facts which we pull out for membership classes and when the pastor preaches his annual "What we Believe" sermon. Other than that, the gospel often has very little impact on our daily lives. If the life-transforming ideas of the gospel are not flowing through our lives into our words and actions toward other people, we are getting the gospel wrong.

We see this, for example, when some churches try to increase the impact of doctrinal statements on people's lives by requiring their teenagers and potential members to memorize the doctrinal statement ... or at least read it as part of every Sunday church service. The common consensus on this practice, however, is that while a creed can be memorized and recited, the practice rarely leads to any real life change. The words can be faithfully spoken while the mind wanders to problems at work, what Mrs. Pilsnick is wearing in church today, and who is going to win the NFL game this afternoon.

A better practice than memorizing and reciting the creeds might involve helping people live out the gospel by taking them out into the community to love and serve others. In this way, we truly learn about the truth of Scripture, the significance of the death and resurrection of Jesus, the importance of sanctification and holiness, and the indwelling of the Holy Spirit. A better practice than catechism and creedal recitation might be service in a community housing project or clearing trash from underneath the bridge where homeless people sleep.[5]

Even among those who can memorize and recite the creed, does it really make that much difference in their lives? Have they really understood the gospel? If one believes all the right things and can sign on the dotted line of the best doctrinal statement that the church has ever written, but their life is full of hatred, greed, and selfishness, have they really understood the essential parts of the gospel? While a person may believe in Jesus for eternal life and glean some important truths from the teachings of Jesus, if they do not live and love like Jesus, have they really understood what Jesus came to show and do?

The answer to such questions is an obvious "No." Yet the way many of our churches are structured today, a person can sign on the dotted line of their church doctrinal statement, and as long as they attend church regularly and put some money in the plate as it passes by, they can usually be a "member in good standing." This is true even if their personal behavior aligns more closely to that of Judas Iscariot than to that of Jesus Christ.

We have all known people who believe all the right things, but are some of the most hateful and hurtful people we have ever met. They are porcupine Christians: they have lots of good points, but they stick anybody who gets too close. Have such Christians really understood the gospel? I think not. They may have believed some of the essential truths of the gospel, and they probably have eternal life, but they have not understood the central focus or entire point of the gospel. As believers in Jesus, we must also follow

---

[5] See Jeremy Myers, *Put Service Back into the Church Service* (Dallas, OR: Redeeming Press, 2013).

Him into a life of love and service to others in this world. The gospel cannot be summarized in a doctrinal statement because statements of belief usually do not also contain statements of behavior, and even if they did, such "lists" soon become legalistic rules, which undermines the gospel even further. So in general, doctrinal statements lead people to think that if they just believe the right things and sign on the dotted line, then they can live any way they want. In such a way, doctrinal statements have gutted the gospel of any real importance or significance in our lives.

Therefore, let us do away with lifeless summaries of the gospel in our doctrinal statements so that we can better lead people into a gospel-filled life of following Jesus to love and serve others. Doctrine can be good, if used as Jesus used it. This is the topic of the next chapter.

DISCUSSION QUESTIONS

1. As a religion, what has Christianity become focused upon?

2. What does our "war on words" cause within Christianity?

3. Though modern Christian may not murder others for having different theological views, what do we do to others instead?

4. Have you ever had a friendship or family relationship end because the other person had different theological views than yourself? Who ended this relationship? If it was you, what why did you end the relationship? Do you feel threatened by their ideas? Do you feel that you could have remained in a relationship with them if they didn't have these other ideas?

5. Why did the church develop doctrinal statements in the first place?

6. What are doctrinal statements intended to create? What do they actually create?

7. Is there one or more aspects of your church's doctrinal statement that has caused some people to leave the church? Is this part of the doctrinal statement truly necessary?

8. Which sort of judgments is the church never supposed to make?

9. What is one reason that we as humans want other people to believe the same way we do?

10. Historically, how do doctrinal statements usually become "accepted?"

11. How do you think the use of doctrinal statements has contributed to the fracture of Christianity into thousands of different denominations?

12. When we set up doctrinal statements to know who is "in" and who is "out," what are we really trying to do?

13. In what way were Emperors and Kings often involved in making doctrinal statements? Why did they involve themselves?

14. Do you believe that people with power and influence play any part in the making of doctrinal statements today? If so, why do they do this?

15. Why were people killed for their beliefs in the past?

16. How does a doctrinal statement or creed kill the creativity of individuals?

17. Through creeds are designed to create unity, what do they actually create? Why?

18. In what ways do doctrinal statements miss the point of the gospel?

19. If the gospel is not a set of ideas to believe in, what is it?

20. Is memorizing a creed the best way to get people to live a more living life toward others? Why or why not?

21. Why does having people sign on the dotted line of a doctrinal statement tell us nothing about how that person lives?

22. If you wanted your child to act lovingly toward others, would you have them (1) Sign a sign a code of conduct and have them memorize rules for good behavior, or (2) Show them how to live with your life and teach them to live in similar ways? Defend your answer.

CHAPTER 8

GOOD DOCTRINE

If doctrinal statements cause so many problems, do they have any positive benefits? Can anything good come out of creeds? Yes; creeds are not all bad. This chapter explains some of the benefits and proper uses of doctrinal statements.

THREE BENEFITS TO DOCTRINAL STATEMENTS

There are at least three positive benefits to doctrinal statements. These benefits allow us to keep using doctrinal statements, but only if we are able to avoid some of the pitfalls and problems of doctrinal statements that were discussed in the previous chapter.

Doctrinal Statements provide a guiding hermeneutic

In some ways, doctrinal statements are a summary of the doctrinal conclusions that Christians of the past have drawn from Scripture. They tell us what various groups have thought to be the key ideas from the Bible. In such a way, they can provide a guide for us in our own study. If we believe that the Holy Spirit has helped guide Christians of the past to know and understand the truth of Scripture, then it makes sense to believe that doctrinal statements can help us in our own understanding and interpretation of Scripture.

For example, most doctrinal statements include the idea that Jesus is fully human and fully divine. Therefore, we must be extremely cautious about any teaching to the contrary, for nearly all Christians throughout church history have held to this belief. Similarly, other points from doctrinal statements often represent key teachings from Scripture and can help guide our own study into Scripture, keeping us within the doctrinal boundaries of Christians from the past.

Doctrinal Statements help people know what to expect

When I listen to a pastor or visit a ministry website, one of the first things I do is look for a doctrinal statement. I want to know where the ministry or teacher is coming from. This doesn't mean that if I don't like their doctrinal statement, I will reject what they say outright. No, I will (usually) still listen to what is said. But knowing where they are coming from doctrinally helps provide perspective on what is taught.

Revealing our doctrinal statement is somewhat like "opening our books" to the public. It shows that we have no secrets, that what we believe is available for all to read, and that what we believe is in line with historic and traditional Christianity. We must not be like Scientologists or some other pseudo-religious group that hides what they believe from the general public and only makes it available to those who undergo some super-secret initiation rite. No, let us be transparent. Publishing a public doctrinal statement helps people know who you are and what you believe.

Doctrinal Statements guide leadership decisions

In a church or ministry setting, you simply cannot have people on the leadership team who have major doctrinal differences with each other. I mean, if the Senior Pastor of a church believes that Jesus is God while the Assistant Pastor believes that Jesus was just an enlightened human, there are going to be problems with how that church functions. A doctrinal statement helps the leadership team stay on the same page.

However, just because a doctrinal statement can be used to restrict who is placed in a position of leadership in a church or ministry, I strongly discourage the use of doctrinal statements as a means of restricting who can attend or participate with the church or ministry in its services and functions. This is when doctrinal statements become dangerous.

Let the Three Benefits Be the Guide

If you decide to use a doctrinal statement, let the three benefits guide you in what to include in your doctrinal statement. After all, the length and complexity of a doctrinal statement is directly proportional to the amount of control, power, abuse, and disunity within the church that the doctrinal statement creates.

So do you really need that point about Seven Day Creationism or the paragraph about the Tribulation and the Millennium? Is the section on Tongues and the Baptism of the Holy Spirit really necessary? Must you really explain that the Five Points of Calvinism are the true gospel as taught by Paul? Is it really that important to clarify that women and homosexuals are not allowed to be pastors in your church? (By the way, I disagree with nearly *all* of these points.)

I used to have a rather long and detailed personal doctrinal statement. Now I simply use the following:

1. Jesus Christ is fully God and fully human.

2. Jesus was crucified on a cross, died, was buried, and rose again physically from the dead, and will return physically in the future to rule and reign over the earth with justice and righteousness.
3. Eternal life is granted by grace alone, through faith alone, in Jesus alone.
4. There will be a future physical resurrection for all who believe in Jesus for eternal life.[1]

This statement is very simple, easily understood, and shows where I fit within the general flow of Christian history and tradition. Hopefully, such a statement does not lead to division and strife, but instead to unity, love, and encouragement to live like Jesus.

So as important as theology and doctrine are and as helpful as doctrinal statements can be in helping the church accomplish its mission, when it comes to defining and defending our doctrine, there is a more excellent way.

A MORE EXCELLENT WAY

If doctrine is not the tie that binds the church together in unity, what is?

In his letters to the Corinthians, Paul corrects numerous practical and doctrinal issues within the church. But at one point, in the middle of dealing with the divisive doctrine of spiritual gifts, and after begging the Corinthian believers to live in unity with

---

[1] See the history and explanation of this doctrinal statement here: https://redeeminggod.com/undoctrinal-statement/

one another, he shows them the key to unity.

The key to unity, says Paul, is not doctrinal precision or even ethical perfection, but love. Though 1 Corinthians 13 is often read at weddings, it has very little to do with the love between a man and a wife, and everything to do with how a church can function as the Body of Christ. The secret is not spiritual gifts, but love. The secret is not prophecy or preaching and teaching, but love. The secret is not accurate knowledge of theology or faith that moves mountains, but love. The secret is not abundant generosity to the poor or becoming a martyr for the faith, but love.

What does this mean for our churches? It means that how we treat one another and what we do for our neighbors matters more than what we write down on our doctrinal statements. Sure, right believing is important, but according to Paul, all the doctrine and theology in the world is worthless if we have not love.

It is true, as many like to point out, that love without truth in not truly love. But those who argue this way are usually just trying to defend their lack of love. It is much easier to sign a doctrinal statement than it is to show love to the sick, the dying, the dirty, and the lost. Love is too hard; that's why we focus on doctrinal statements instead. In *What's Wrong with the World*, G. K. Chesterton wrote, "The Christian ideal has not been tried and found wanting. It has been found difficult, and left untried." But we must try, for the alternative is only more of the same: more doctrinal statements, more division, and more disunity.

And let us not say that love and unity are impossible, that the gulf if too wide, the divisions too severe, the doctrinal differences too great. Since the divisions first began nearly 1700 years ago, the church has never really tried to reunite. But if we could unite, if we could love one another, if we could agree that love for others was more important than being right about the rapture, then maybe the church would stop dividing over doctrine and start showing the world what the love of God really looks like. In his book *Small Faith, Great God*, N. T. Wright wrote "The world has yet to see what God will do through a worldwide church whose members love one another."[2]

Uniting together with other believers does not mean we have to ignore doctrine, but only that we put doctrine in its rightful place. Doctrine must amplify rather than restrict our love for others. Love can be built into the doctrinal statement. Each point in the statement must bleed with love. Love from God, love for God, and love for others must be evident everywhere when we talk about what we believe. Maybe along with the doctrinal statement, a church or organization could also develop a "To Do" Statement. They would not only have a statement of what they believe, but also a statement of how they behave. The "Simple Way" in Philadelphia has both statements. According to Shane Claiborne, they have a doctrinal statement to prove they are not a cult and they have a statement of practices so people know they are not *just* believers.[3] Churches, communities, and organizations that follow similar practices reveal that they are centered on both truth and love.

None of this means that we sacrifice truth on the altar of love. Far from it! Instead, we realign ourselves to what truth really is, and where truth can be found.

---

[2] N. T. Wright, *Small Faith, Great God* (Downers Grove: IVP, 2010), 137.

[3] Shane Claiborne, *The Irresistible Revolution* (Grand Rapids: Zondervan, 2006), 125.

WHAT IS THE TRUTH?

We often become convinced that truth is found in a doctrinal statement, or in the Bible, and while truth can be found in such places, Scripture and doctrinal statements themselves are not the source of truth. They are both pointers or witnesses to the truth, but are not themselves "the truth."

Let me put this another way. Everybody who has a doctrinal statement believes that their doctrinal statement accurately represents the teaching of Scripture. But since not all doctrinal statements agree, this means that not all doctrinal statements accurately represent the teachings of Scripture. Since not all doctrinal statements agree, some points on some doctrinal statements must be wrong, and we must not be so arrogant to think that our chosen doctrinal statement is 100% accurate while everybody else is in error.

The same goes for Scripture. When we say that our doctrinal statements just follow the teachings of Scripture, what we really mean is that our doctrinal statements follow our *understanding* of Scripture. Yet our understanding of Scripture may not be the actual teachings of Scripture in every case.

This brings us to the nature of truth. While I do think that there are some things we can know with absolute certainty, many of the ideas found on most doctrinal statements do not fall into this category. And yet, because they get written into a formal "doctrinal statement" the words of the statement become set in stone, and soon, we become slaves to the statements. They surround us with walls and bind us with chains until we are no longer free.

It is much better, I believe, to think of truth not as something that has been achieved and can be summarized on a piece of paper, but as a target to shoot for or a goal to accomplish. Truth is not something that we have already obtained, but something that we strive to obtain.

And what is at the center of this target? What is the goal that we strive for? What is the truth?

Simply this: the truth is Jesus Christ. He is the Way, the Truth, and the Life (John 14:6). In Him is Truth.

Some point to John 17:17 as proof that Jesus wants people to look to Scripture as the primary source of truth. In this verse, Jesus prays that God will "Sanctify them by Your truth. Your word is truth." But in the surrounding context, and in the Gospel of John as a whole, Jesus is identified as "the Word" from heaven which has come into the world, the Word from God which has revealed God's truth. Jesus is the truth. Jesus is the focus. Jesus is the target. Jesus is the goal. Jesus is the Word which sanctifies us. So if you want to center your life and ministry on truth, center it on Jesus.

I don't mean that our doctrinal statement should emphasize Jesus. This is just doctrinal sleight of hand where we substitute Jesus for ideas about Jesus, and think they are the same. They aren't. We must be centered, not around a statement, but around a Savior. Not around a creed, but around Christ. Not around some list of beliefs but around lives built on the pattern of Jesus.

In chasing after unity in the truth, what we must strive for is not unity in agreement, but unity in love. This is the New Testament way. Though finer points of theology can be discussed and debated, at the end of the day we must all be able to say, "I love you still."

I am of the conviction that where there is no love, there is no truth. Truth, if is known, treats others with love, even when they disagree. Look at God, after all. He knows everything, and as a result, loves everyone.

The goal of doctrine, discussion, and theological debate is not to make us more right, but to make us more like Jesus. As we learn from each other, we should be moving ever closer to the center, which is Jesus Christ. And the closer we get to the center, not only do we understand more, but we also love more. For Jesus, who is Truth, is also perfect Love.

As we grow closer to Him we grow closer to each other. So discard your doctrinal statements that so easily entangle, and run with perseverance after Jesus, the author and perfector of our faith.

DISCUSSION QUESTIONS

1. Describe the three positive uses of doctrinal statements. Can you think of any others?

2. If you were to write your own doctrinal statement, which ideas would you include? Which items might you exclude, even if you believe them to be true? Why did you make these choices?

3. What is it that is supposed to bind Christians together? Do doctrinal statements accomplish this?

4. Consider N. T. Wright's quote: "The world has yet to see what God will do through a worldwide church whose mem-

bers love one another." How is the church doing in this vision? What sorts of things might help us accomplish it?

5. What is one Truth all Christians can believe in? What one Truth should hold our focus? How do we go about focusing our eyes on this Truth?

6. Have you ever stopped being friends with someone or hanging out with someone because they had different beliefs than you? Why did you do this? What is stopping you from calling them up right now to set a time to reconnect? If you do reconnect, can you commit to loving them despite your differences of opinion?

PART IV: LET PRAYER MEETINGS CEASE

We have enough people who pray, who attend meetings and services. And more than enough people who argue about what they believe to be right or wrong. But of doers, heaven has not enough. There are not enough people who grasp that in the first place it is not knowledge, or doctrine, or preaching, that is lacking. What is lacking is right living.
—Christoph Blumhardt

When I was a pastor, we held a "Men's Prayer Meeting" on Wednesday night. One evening an Elder shared a prayer request about Edwin. Edwin was a retired pastor from another city and was moving into our town the following Wednesday, and this Elder wanted us to pray that Edwin's transition would be smooth and that he would be welcomed to the community. So this is what we prayed for.

The following week, after we all showed up for the Wednesday prayer meeting, I announced that I had a great answer to prayer to share with the group. "Remember last week how we prayed that Edwin's transition to the area would be smooth?" I said. "Well, he arrived in town this afternoon and is moving into his house tonight. And guess what? Seven men from the church showed up to help him unload the moving truck."

"Really, pastor? That's great! Who was it?"

"Us. Let's go."

"But ... but ... our prayer meeting!"

"Tonight, we are answering our own prayers. I'll meet you there."

And we went.

Our prayers weren't always answered this way though. Many of our prayers went unanswered. I still remember praying week after week, month after month, that the people who lived around the church and right across the street from the church would meet Jesus and start attending our church. By the time I left that church, not a single one of them had darkened the door of our church building.

Looking back now, however, I regret that I never once darkened the door of their house. I wanted them to come meet us, but I never once went to meet them. Not once did I knock on their door to introduce myself and ask how we as the community church might serve them. Not once did I seek to become an answer to our own prayers. I remember being frustrated that God was not bringing more bodies to our church, but I now wonder if God was ever frustrated that I was not taking my body to their homes.

You probably already grasp the point of this chapter. I believe that quite often when we cry out to God, saying, "God! Why aren't you answering my prayers?" God says, "Why aren't you? I'm trying to answer your prayers, but you won't go!"

Prayer, I believe, is not primarily something to say to God in a silent room by yourself or with others, but is the things you say to God while on the way to serving others. Prayer meetings are not a time to dump all our needs or download the desires of our hearts onto God, but are instead times for us to ask God's blessing on the service we are about to perform for others, or to listen to God's heart for the other things He wants us to do. Prayer is not about creating a checklist for God, but a checklist for ourselves. If we want to see God answer more of our prayers, we must seek to be the answer to more of our prayers.

Yet to do this, we must first escape some of the traditional prayer practices that are common in the church today. The following two chapters discuss some of the problems with modern prayer meetings and then suggest some ways for us to properly pray today. If you want to read more on this topic, try my book, *What is Prayer?*

CHAPTER 9

PROBLEM PRAYERS

If you have been to prayer meetings, you have probably heard several different types of prayer. Some of these prayer practices are quite common in the church, but are rarely questioned or challenged. Below are a few of my "favorites."

FIVE "BAD HABIT" PRAYERS

First, there are the prayers of liturgical Christianity where people pray written and memorized prayers. These prayers usually come from Scripture and tradition. The Lord's Prayer is a great example. While saying this prayer can be meaningful and helpful, it can sometimes degenerate into a jumbled string of words where the person praying simply tries to get through it as fast as possible. It doesn't really matter if others understand what is said or not, or if the person praying really means the words.

In some cases, it seems that the only thing that matters is the words themselves regardless of whether or not there is understanding and comprehension. When this happens, it sounds something like this:

Ourfatherwhoartinheavenhallowedbythynamethykingdomcometheywillbedoneonearthasitisinheavengiveusthisdayourdailybreadandforgiveusourtresspassesasweforgivethosewhotresspassagainstusforthineisthekingdomandthepowerandthegloryforeverandeveramen.

In such cases, I sometimes imagine God saying to such people, "Whoa there! Slow down! I like that prayer, but I can't understand a word of what you're saying!" God does understand what is being said, of course, but He doesn't care for such prayers because there is no focus on relational communication in praying this way. Those who pray this way reveal a mindset which believes that prayers are like a magic incantation, where the only thing that matters is that you say the words.

I sometimes think that this is what Jesus might have had in mind when He criticized some people in Matthew 6:7 for babbling their prayers, thinking they will be heard for their many words. It is not the words God cares about, and especially not how fast we can get them out.

The reference in Matthew 6:7 to babbling prayers brings up another type of prayer you might hear in a prayer meeting. In this type of prayer, the person seems to forget what they are praying about, or they are not sure how to pray for the request, or maybe they just want it to sound like they are really connecting with God in their prayer. Regardless of the motive, right in the middle of their prayer, they transition from praying in English to "praying in tongues." At least, that's what they call it. If you have ever heard someone speak in tongues, it sounds more like baby gibberish than an actual language.

As you can probably guess, I myself have never spoken in tongues, and I have no desire to do so. At least, not the way it is done in most Pentecostal circles. There were many times in seminary when I facetiously asked God for the "gift of tongues, but only in the languages of Greek and Hebrew." I suppose technically, this would be the "gift of the translation of tongues." But God never granted that request and through hard work and lots of study, I got mostly B's in Hebrew and Greek.

Personally, I do think that the spiritual gift of tongues is still in use today, but I think it is primarily used in mission's work to help spread the gospel to unreached people groups. Therefore, speaking in tongues is not something we should expect to see in church prayer meetings, and especially not when everyone present speaks the same language. As Paul said, it is better to speak five words that people understand than 10,000 words in a tongue which nobody understands (1 Cor 14:19).

A third type of prayer occurs when a few words or phrases are repeated over and over throughout the entire prayer. Sometimes these words are "Glory to God! Hallelujah!" Other times they are "Father God," "Holy Jesus," "Bless Your Name, Oh Lord" or some combination and variation of these phrases. Usually, while the person is praying out loud, they will inject these words at the beginning of every sentence, and sometimes right in the middle of a sentence.

In church prayer meetings, we usually don't think anything is amiss with this sort of praying because it is so common. And while this sort of praying is not quite as strange as speaking in tongues, if it was ever carried over into a real-world conversation with another human being, it would sound completely bizarre. Imagine that instead of praying to "Father God," two men, Theo and Andrew, are having a conversation where Andrew repeats Theo's name every few words. Here is how this conversation might sound:

Theo: Hey Andrew! How have you …

Andrew: Oh Theo, I thank you for letting me come into your presence today, Theo, and Theo, I ask that you bless me today, Theo. For I am your servant, Theo, and come before you with nothing but an outstretched hand, oh Theo, hoping that you might, Theo, in your glory, Theo, and out of your grace, Theo, see fit to listen to my needs, Theo, and hear my requests, Theo, and grant them, Theo, according to your mercy, Theo.

Theo: Uhhhh …

Andrew: And Theo, there are many people in this place, Theo, who have many burdens, Theo, and they come before you with many sins, Theo, which you, oh Theo, in your infinite wisdom, Theo, already know about, Theo. And we thank you, Theo, that because of your blood, Theo, shed for us, Theo, we might enter your presence, Theo, with boldness, Theo, before your throne of grace, Theo …

Theo: You can stop saying my name now. I'm not going to forget it.

Andrew: Oh Theo, Theo, Theo, Theo, Theo, Theo, Theo. We love your holy name, oh Theo. For in your name, Theo, there is strength, oh Theo, and power, oh Theo, and might, oh Theo, and glory! In your great name, Theo, we cast out evil spirits, Theo, and bind the enemy, Theo …

Have you ever heard prayers like this? Where "Father God" or "Lord Jesus" is mentioned every third or fourth word? This sort of prayer goes on for a while, and the person praying develops quite a rhythm, until pretty soon, those listening to the prayer start whispering or even shouting the name of God also.

Granted, this method of prayer works great if you want the crowd to start enthusiastically shouting "Amen!" Furthermore, those who pray this way are also usually thought of as eloquent and energetic prayer warriors. But if prayer is actually about having a conversation with God about what is important to Him and to us, I am not sure that this is the best way to pray.[1]

Maybe the worst type of prayer, however, is when the person praying goes back and forth between talking to God and talking to Satan. When I hear these sorts of prayers, I often wonder, "Who are they praying to?" Here is an example of how these prayers sound:

> God, we thank you for your many answers to prayer this week, and—Devil! I rebuke you in the name of Jesus—and God, may you guide us and direct us this week according to your will—Satan! I bind you and cast you out with the authority of the name of Jesus!—and God, we especially want to lift up to you today Sister Maynard—Get out Satan! Get out! Leave her alone!—who is struggling with the flu this week—Evil spirit of the flu, get out of her! Leave foul demon!—may you use your power and might to restore her to health ...

I doubt God likes to share our prayers to Him in this way. Half of the prayer is a conversation with Him, and the other half is a conversation with the devil.

---

[1] See J. D. Myers, *What is Prayer?* (Dallas, OR: Redeeming Press, 2019). This book is all about how to pray to God as if you were having a conversation with any other person. If you can talk to someone else, then you already know how to properly talk to God.

One last example of a poor prayer method is when people use big words in their prayers even though they have no clue what the words mean. I recently heard a man pray for his meal by saying, "I thank you, Oh Lord God Almighty, for this bread which thou hast bestowed upon us from the fruit of your loins …" I cringed when I heard this and I think God laughed at it too.

Where do people learn to pray in all these ways? Not from Scripture, not from life, not from logic, and definitely not from having conversations with other people, for nobody talks to one another in any of these ways. There is primarily one place where people learn to pray this way. They learn these bad prayer habits in church prayer meetings.

In this chapter, I encourage Christians to pray more and attend prayer meetings less. I intend to show how prayer meetings typically do not help us accomplish God's mission in the world, but hinder it instead. We will look at a few pitfalls of prayer meetings, and address a few passages that teach about prayer. The next chapter will suggest some ways that churches and Christians can pray with a missional and kingdom-focused mindset.

PITFALLS OF PRAYER MEETINGS

Please do not misunderstand. Prayer meetings are not all bad. For every prayer you hear that fits the poor examples described above, you will hear hundreds of prayers in prayer meetings that are genuine, heart-felt, meaningful conversations with God about Who He is, what He has done, and how we would like Him to help us live life and serve Him better.

Nevertheless, even though many of the prayers in prayer meetings are meaningful and heart-felt, there are still numerous pitfalls to prayer meetings. For example, have you ever noticed how the true "prayer warriors" of the typical church never seem to come to "Prayer meetings"? Have you ever wondered why?

Have you ever thought it odd that when you ask your pastor to pray for a pressing need in your life, he writes it down and then says, "I'll bring it up at the prayer meeting this Wednesday"?

Again, has it ever seemed strange to you that although there can be dozens of people out in the community loving others, serving the poor, meeting needs, and helping the homeless, the "truly spiritual people" are those who come to church on Wednesday night for the prayer meeting where they pray for the poor, the homeless, and the other needs of the community? Why are the ones who pray about these needs more spiritual than the ones who actually go meet the needs?

And then there are all the sermons and slogans about how the church advances on its knees, how real men are kneeling men, and how the attendance at prayer meeting reveals the true health and vitality of the church. Aside from the fact that these ideas are simply not true, it seems that these sermons and slogans really don't get people to pray more, but simply guilt them into showing up for another meeting in the church building.

This brings up the main reason to let prayer meetings cease: Even when prayer meetings are healthy and people don't learn bad prayer habits, they still teach people bad theology about prayer. Rather than showing people how to pray without ceasing, prayer meetings teach people that there is a time and a place and a particular method for prayer. Specifically, prayer meetings give people the impression that prayer involves sitting in a circle, folding our hands, closing our eyes, and bowing our heads. Prayer meetings teach people that prayer is more effective when there are several people gathered in a room praying about something. They teach people that aside from attending church on Sunday morning, the next most important thing in their life as a follower of Jesus is attending church on Wednesday night.

But none of this is actually true!

Prayer *is* vital, just as gathering together with other believers for prayer is vital, but prayer does not require a regularly-scheduled prayer meeting as practiced in some churches today. Learning how to pray, learning what to pray for, and learning how prayer is answered is best accomplished in other ways. This is the topic of the next chapter.

DISCUSSION QUESTIONS

1. What do you like about prayer? What do you dislike? Why?

2. Do you struggle with using any of the five types of prayer discussed in this chapter? Where do you think you learned this type of prayer? Is there something you think you can do to break the habit of praying in this way?

3. Have you heard others pray in any of the five types of "bad habit" prayers? Do you find them somewhat annoying? Why or why not?

4. If you could design a way of talking with God that felt "right" to you, what would it look like?

5. Which pitfall of prayer meetings do you most agree with? Why?

6. Which pitfall of prayer meetings do you disagree with? Why?

7. What do you think prayer was meant to teach us?

8. Can you think of a prayer request you've recently heard from someone else to which you could have supplied the answer to that prayer request?

CHAPTER 10

HOW SHOULD WE PRAY?

One of the best ways to think about prayer is to view it as simply having a conversation with God. If someone can talk to a spouse, coworker, friend, or neighbor, they can talk to God in prayer. No special training or vocabulary is needed, nor is any special posture and location required. Whatever you would talk to a friend about, you can talk to God about. Wherever you might speak to a friend, you can speak to God. You do not need to be gathered together with others, though sometimes that is helpful for the sake of the conversation. You do not have to be in a certain building or room, though sometimes, that also is helpful so you can focus on what is being said.

Even still, some people are uncertain of what to say when they pray. After all, having a conversation with God seems different than having a conversation with a friend. So it is helpful to give people some ideas of the sorts of things that can be said in conversation with God. All of us want to pray, and so thankfully, God has included in Scripture numerous examples of what to pray for and how to pray. If you are like the disciples of Jesus and are asking, "Lord, teach us to pray," then consider your request granted.

PASSAGES ON PRAYER

Below are four passages that some people find helpful as they learn to converse with God.

The Disciples' Prayer

The passage that many people think of as "The Lord's Prayer" might better be called "The Disciples' Prayer." Near the middle of the three years of Jesus' ministry, His disciples noticed that He spent a lot of time in prayer. They wanted to pray as He prayed, so they came to Jesus and asked Him to teach them to pray (Luke 11:1). They did not ask because they did not know how to pray, for the Jewish people had many daily and weekly times of prayer. But most of these Jewish prayers were memorized and recited. They were formal, ceremonial prayers for particular events and holidays. The disciples noticed that Jesus prayed differently; He seemed to talk with God as a man talks to a friend, or a Father. For Jesus, prayer was natural and normal, and the disciples wanted to pray this way as well.

So Jesus taught His disciples how to pray (Luke 11:2-4; Matt 6:9-13). In doing so, He lists several examples of what they could say to God. What Jesus provided in "The Disciples' Prayer" was not another written, formulaic prayer for them to memorize and recite, but instead provided a series of topics and ideas to help them know what to talk to God about. Jesus was not telling His disciples *exactly* the words they should use when they prayed, but was instead giving them *examples* of the sorts of things they could pray for. He gave them broad themes and ideas.

And what are the themes and ideas that Jesus instructed His disciples to pray? They include giving praise and glory to God, requests for the rule and reign of God to expand on earth, petitions for God to provide for our daily needs, that He would forgive us for the ways we have failed to keep His will, and a request for protection from further failures. These are all basic requests and can be prominent themes of any person's prayer life.

The Lord's Prayer

The true "Lord's Prayer" is found in John 17, which is the prayer that Jesus prayed in the Upper Room with His disciples at the conclusion of their last supper together. Though the Gospels frequently record Jesus going off by Himself to pray, this is the only recorded prayer of Jesus of any length which provides an indication of the sort of things Jesus might have said when He prayed.

Scholars have long noted that the prayer is divided into three basic sections. Jesus prays for Himself (17:1-5), then for His disciples (17:6-19), and finally for all who would believe in Him (17:20-26). Much can be said about the content of Jesus' prayer, especially that the primary prayer request of Jesus for all who would believe in Him is that we would be unified (17:21). But my purpose here is not to analyze and explain the prayer of Jesus as much as it is to simply look at how Jesus prayed.

Notice first the posture of Jesus. The text does not tell us if Jesus was sitting, standing, or reclining (though reclining on the floor was the typical way of eating meals and conversing afterwards in first century Middle Eastern culture). One thing is for sure though: Jesus definitely was not bowing His head, folding His hands, or closing His eyes. To the contrary, the text says He "lifted up His eyes to heaven" (17:1), which indicates that His eyes were open and His head was raised. Nevertheless, even this is not the "God-approved" posture of prayer. It is not as if such things as kneeling or standing, arms up or arms down, eyes open or eyes closed make any difference in whether or not God hears and answers our prayers. If God is concerned about any sort of posture in our prayer, it is the posture of our hearts, which no one can see but Him alone.

One other striking detail about the prayer of Jesus is that He begins by praying for Himself. How often have we been told in sermons and books on prayer that we must not begin with ourselves, but instead, begin with adoration of God, and thanksgiving for what He has done? I have not only heard such sermons; I have preached them myself! For example, I once preached a sermon on the ACTS method of prayer, using the acronym ACTS as a pattern for prayer: Adoration, Confession, Thanksgiving, Supplication. In this patter, the requests for self and others come last. Yet when Jesus prays, the first thing He prays about is Himself. Of course, this was no selfish prayer, for even though He begins with Himself, notice what He prays for: He prays that He would glorify the Father. So really, this first prayer request is not exactly about Jesus, but about glorifying God the Father. This is a great thing to pray for yourself, because bringing glory to God the father is one of the primary reasons we are here on earth.

Jesus however, does not *only* pray for Himself as some of us are guilty of doing (myself included!), but spends most of His prayer focusing on others. I think most of us are familiar with the concept of praying for other people, but even then, Jesus' prayer is not about their health or wealth (which is what our prayer requests for others seem to focus on ... "Heal their disease ... help them get a job"). Instead, Jesus prays that others would remain faithful to God and in unity with each another. I don't think God minds hearing prayers for Aunt Mabel's bunion, our neighbor's dog, and how the rent is overdue, especially when these are issues that really do concern us, but I do believe that it would be wise for all Christians to develop a broader vision for prayer than how we can use it to tell God about our aches and pains and bills.

Notice also what Jesus does *not* pray for. Nowhere is the needless repetition of the names of God. Nowhere is any attempt to ward off the devil. Nowhere is any flowery and fancy language to impress others with His advanced holiness. In fact, there is almost nothing that sets this prayer apart from any other conversation Jesus has with any of His disciples elsewhere in the Gospels. His conversation with God sounds pretty much just like a conversation He might have with Peter, Matthew, or John. For Jesus, communicating with God was just like communicating with others; no special language was needed.

This is the main thing we can learn from the prayer of Jesus in John 17. As I read the prayer, it sounds like a small part of a much longer conversation Jesus has been having with God for a very long time. As such, Jesus does not appear to have the need to fit everything in, follow a prayer outline, use any special language, remember any prayer requests, or even begin and end the prayer with a flowery introduction and conclusion. He simply transitions from talking to His disciples to talking to God. One second He is looking at His disciples and speaking to them, and the next second He is looking at God and speaking to Him. His tone and language and posture and even the content of what He is saying does not really change. For Jesus, prayer is just continuing a conversation with God. It is as if God is right in the room with the disciples, and simply with a turn of the head, Jesus includes God in the conversation they have all been having together.

This is the best way to think about prayer. Prayer is nothing more (and nothing less) than a conversation with God who is in the room with all of us. When understood this way, prayer becomes much less of a mystery about how to pray and what to pray for and who can pray and where to pray, and much more like a conversation we have in everyday life. If you can talk with a friend, you can talk to God. That is how Jesus prayed, and how we can pray too.[1]

Paul's Prayers

But what about Paul's prayers? Are they also a small glimpse or window into a much longer conversation with God? I think so. While there are few examples of Paul *actually* praying in the New Testament, Paul's written statements about his prayers almost sound as if they were prayers themselves (See Rom 15:5-6, 13; Eph 1:16-19; 3:16-19; Php 1:9-11; Col 1:9-12; 2 Thess 1:11-12). If someone desires written prayers in Scripture to help guide their own prayer life, the prayers of Paul are good places to start.

Many of the recorded prayer requests of Paul are nearly identical to the recorded prayer requests of Jesus in John 17. Both Jesus and Paul pray that believers would glorify God through faithful obedience and grow in unity with each other. One other similarity is that just as we saw with Jesus, Paul does not use any special language or terminology in his prayers. The very things Paul writes about in his letters are the things he prays about to God, using the same ideas, language, and style. Paul's communication with God sounds no different than his communication

---

[1] See J. D. Myers, *What is Prayer?* (Dallas, OR: Redeeming Press, 2019).

with humans.

This idea emphasizes the truth once again that prayer is best viewed as a conversation with God. While it is not necessarily wrong to have set patterns, times, places, and requests for prayer, it is highly unlikely that you do this with any of your other conversation partners in life, and hence, you should probably not converse with God in this fashion either.

One reason many people struggle with prayer is because it becomes boring and repetitious. We say the same things in the same way over and over and over. But any conversation would get boring when the same thing is repeated dozens (or hundreds) of times. So also with prayer. Just as conversations with people get dull and boring if we talk about the same things all the time and always in the same order, so also conversation with God can get dull and boring if we always come to Him with the same prayers, the same items, the same requests, always in the same order.

When we talk with God, we can talk to Him just as we would any other person. This is what both Jesus and Paul did in their prayers, and this method of praying will make it real, meaningful, and lively. Sometimes the conversations are short; sometimes they are long. Sometimes they are heated with debate and disagreement; sometimes they are full of praise and love. Sometimes more can be said simply by remaining silent. All of this is very well illustrated when we look at the Book of Psalms as being a book of written prayers.

The Book of Psalms

Many people think of the Book of Psalms as a Book of Songs. That is true, but the Psalms are not simply songs, but are closer to prayers that were intended to be sung. Specifically, they were prayers that were to be sung when Israel worshiped God in the temple, during their annual festivals, and in both private and corporate times of worship. This is not so different than most "worship songs" of today. If you listen to the words of most worship choruses, many of them are "prayerful" in their words and themes. So also with the Psalms.

One great thing about the Psalms is that they reflect the full range of human emotions. While many of the Psalms are about giving praise and honor to God, or calling on the people to faithfully love and serve Him, some of the Psalms reflect the heart of a person who is angry with God and tells Him so (Psa 10:1; 22:1; 42:9; 74:1, 11). Other times the Psalmist is angry at people, and tells God about this as well, to the point of asking God to destroy his enemies (Psa 54:5; 79:10; 143:12). Sometimes the Psalms are quite long (Psa 119); other times they consist of only a sentence or two (Psa 117). Occasionally they use repetition (Psa 136).

As a result, the Book of Psalms is a wonderful tutorial on how the people of God can pray. When people wonder about what sorts of things they can and should pray for, or what type of language and words to use when communicating with God, it is often not enough to just tell them that they can have a conversation with God just like with any other person. For some, this seems too informal. So it is often a good idea to recommend the Book of Psalms as a helpful guide in learning how to pray and what to pray for. As people pray through the Psalms, they learn that pretty much anything can be said to God and any emotion is welcomed by Him. When it comes to prayer, there are no taboo topics or emotions.

Once again, this is just like our real relationships in life. Our genuine relationships and meaningful friendships are the ones where we interact with each other in an honest and open manner. We share emotions, feelings, and ideas without fear of being judged. Where this freedom does not exist, there are no true relationships.

So why do we so often hold back in our prayers? Why are we afraid to speak to God as a man speaks to a close friend? Why do we think God will be offended if we really tell Him what is on our hearts or what we think about Him and how He is running the world? Rather than be afraid of saying the wrong thing in prayer, we must learn to boldly approach the throne of grace and speak to God like we would speak to any other close friend. This is one of the things the Psalms teaches us to do. When we pray the Psalms, we learn to express all of our feelings and emotions to God, just as we do with any true friend.

Just as our conversations with others cover the whole spectrum of emotions and subjects, praying the Psalms helps us see that prayer is an ongoing and open conversation with God. Sometimes we are careful with our words and ideas. Other times we don't hold back.

This concept we have seen from the prayers of Jesus, Paul, and the Psalms about prayer being an ongoing conversation with God helps us understand what Paul meant when He instructed the Thessalonian believers to "pray without ceasing."

PRAY WITHOUT CEASING

In 1 Thessalonians 5:17, Paul instructed his readers to "pray without ceasing." Many Christians have struggled with how this can actually be accomplished in their life. But this struggle comes from a basic misunderstanding about *how* to pray. If prayer is a set time and place where we go into a particular room, get down on our knees, fold our hands, bow our heads, close our eyes, and say certain things to God, it is nearly impossible to follow Paul's instruction. How could one possibly do this nonstop and still go to work, hang out with family and friends, eat meals, or sleep at night?

Yet some Christians try. You will hear or read some pastors and spiritual leaders teaching that prayer is a spiritual discipline, and while the new believer may only pray for five minutes a day, the mature and more dedicated Christians will spend more time in prayer, so that the truly spiritual prayer warrior might pray for several hours a day. Martin Luther once said that he tried to spend two hours every day in prayer, but if he was really busy, he would spend three.

This sort of mentality was found in the Desert Fathers who went out into the wilderness so they could devote more time to prayer. Today, people go on "prayer retreats" for similar purposes.

In all such cases, nobody claims to be praying without ceasing. They sleep, eat, run errands, and talk to other people. Though they may pray *more,* they do not pray nonstop. This, however, is not due to a lack of trying, but rather due to a poor understanding of prayer. As long as one has a formalized definition of prayer that requires a certain posture and way of speaking, then praying without ceasing is impossible.

Do not misunderstand. I am not against formalized times, places, and postures of prayer. I think Jesus might have had all of these. We do read that He often got up very early in the morning and went out to a solitary place to pray (Mark 1:35). But it would be wrong to think that these were the only times Jesus prayed. Jesus understood what it meant to pray without ceasing, and these early morning times of prayer were a small part of His overall prayer life. John 5:19-20 best summarizes this where Jesus states that He only does what He sees the Father doing. Jesus was in constant communication and imitation of God, even when conscious thoughts and words were being directed toward God.

Praying without ceasing requires us to think about prayer as we have seen in the recorded prayers of Jesus, Paul, and the Psalms. If prayer is an ongoing conversation we are having with God, and if God is with us always, then we can always be in conversation with Him. Constant prayer is a watchfulness or attentiveness to the presence of God in everything we do. Constant prayer is like taking a long walk with God over the entirety of one's life. When you are on a long walk with someone else, you may not talk the entire time, but you nevertheless communicate with each other by the way you walk together. This is how to think of the life-long conversation with God that we call prayer.

And lest we forget, silence is an important part of any true conversation. Sometimes there is a lot to say, and sometimes it is enough to just be in each other's presence. Sometimes long periods of silence are necessary to think carefully about what to say or to process what has been said to you. Communication doesn't stop just because the words do. And when you are in a relationship with someone, though it is nice to sit down for a long talk on a particular subject, you can also casually discuss issues as you run errands, take a walk, eat meals, or watch television.

When we view prayer as a conversation with a God who is always present, it opens up a whole new realm of freedom in prayer. You no longer have to feel guilty about not spending enough time in prayer. You no longer have to begin and end each prayer with certain words, because in an ongoing conversation there is no beginning or end. You no longer have to remember to pray about something; you can just start talking about it with God right then and there. If you find yourself in a bad situation, you no longer have to think, "I should have prayed for protection this morning," for you can pray for protection right then. Even a word or two will do: "God! Help!"

In these ways and so many others, your prayer life can be transformed, from a tired and boring religious duty that you try to fit in to your busy day, into a vibrant and inspiring ongoing conversation with a living and powerful God who is always by your side. You say "Good morning" when you wake up, and "Good night" when you fall asleep. You thank Him for the taste of your coffee in your mug, and praise Him for the beauty of the frost on the grass. You discuss with him the problems you are facing with your daughter, and your worry about the meeting with your boss at work. And when you sin (as you will every day), you don't need to fear that God was scared off by what you did or too offended to talk with you any longer. No, He's seen and heard it all before. So you laugh with God about your weakness and thank Him for the forgiveness He has already offered by His grace through Jesus Christ. And then you continue your day with Him walking by your side.

This is how we pray without ceasing. It is an ongoing conversation with God. Incidentally, this is also how we learn to pray according to the will of God.

PRAY ACCORDING TO THE WILL OF GOD

Once we understand that talking with God is like talking to a person who is with us always, and that Scripture (especially the Psalms) can be a helpful guide in learning what to pray for and how to pray, all of the mystery disappears from praying according to the will of God.

To see what it means to pray according to the will of God, it might first be helpful to look at some of the texts that mention this topic. Several passages in Scripture have caused a lot of problems over the years regarding prayer. Here are three of the more prominent:

> Ask, and it will be given to you; seek, and you will find; knock, and it will be opened to you. For everyone who asks receives, and he who seeks finds, and to him who knocks it will be opened. Or what man is there among you who, if his son asks for bread, will give him a stone? Or if he asks for a fish, will he give him a serpent? If you then, being evil, know how to give good gifts to your children, how much more will your Father who is in heaven give good things to those who ask Him! (Matt 7:7-11).

> If you abide in Me, and My words abide in you, you will ask what you desire, and it shall be done for you (John 15:7).

> Now this is the confidence that we have in Him, that if we ask anything according to His will, He hears us. And if we know that He hears us, whatever we ask, we know that we have the petitions that we have asked of Him (1 John 5:14-15).

While these texts do teach the importance of praying according to the will of God, what is often missed about these texts is that the context of these verses contain information about abiding with Jesus Christ and living in fellowship with Him.

To abide with Christ means to remain, to dwell, to stay with

Christ. Abiding with Christ, or remaining with Him, is a prominent theme in John 14-17, as well as the first letter of John, and in both contexts it seems that to abide with Christ simply means to always be aware of His presence. To abide with Christ is to be in constant communication with Him, to understand that He is always with you. It means to talk with Him and go through life with Him as you would someone who is always by your side. The prerequisite to praying according to the will of God is abiding or remaining in a close relationship with Jesus Christ.

As we develop this constant awareness and the constant communication that goes with it, and as we learn to pray the Scriptures, we find that our prayer life changes. What we pray for and how we pray also changes. We pray for things that are according to the truths found in Scripture, and for the things that are part of a long-running conversation with God. In this conversation, He challenges our motives and requests and helps us focus on what we really need. He shows us what would be best for His purposes and mission in the world.

As we pray conversationally with God through our close relationship with Jesus Christ, we can know that He is informing, guiding, and refining our prayer requests so that we pray according to His will. And when we pray according to His will, we know that He hears us, and we know that we have what we asked of Him. When we pray according to His will, it is guaranteed that our prayers get answered.

Praying according to the will of God is not that mysterious or difficult when you are in close fellowship with Jesus Christ and in an ongoing communication with God by the indwelling Holy Spirit. When we live this way, our prayer requests will naturally be in accordance to God's will because we know what it is that

God wants of us and in this world. Praying according to God's will often leads us to live according to God's will, which in turn can provide the guaranteed answers to prayer.

While this concept of praying according to the will of God by abiding in Christ may initially seem nebulous or difficult to comprehend, we all practice something similar in our day-to-day lives. We all live in close connection to various people on a daily basis. This may be family members such as parents, children, or a spouse, but it can also include coworkers, neighbors, or friends.

When you first begin to develop these relationships, you may not know much about the other person, such as what they want, enjoy, expect, or desire, or even how they feel about you. And so it is sometimes difficult initially to live in a way that is mutually beneficial and satisfying for both of you. But the longer you live with the other person and interact with them on a daily basis, the more tuned in you become to their likes, hopes, dreams, and desires. Just as they over time how to best show you love and respect, so also, you learn how to show them love and respect. Eventually, as you grow closer and closer, you don't have to wonder about what the other person wants or even what they are thinking, for you automatically know. It is almost as if your mind has become one with theirs.

This is exactly how it works with praying according to God's will. As we live and dwell with Jesus Christ (abide in Him), we begin to learn what He wants and desires for this world and for our life. As we read and study Scripture, as we walk and talk with Jesus, we automatically develop "the mind of Christ" (1 Cor 2:16; Php 2:5-8) so that we begin to think about things just as Jesus does. And since Jesus is of one mind with the Father, so also, as we abide in Christ, we will be of one mind with the Father also.

As this happens, when we pray, we will be praying for the things Jesus would pray for, and therefore, we will be praying according to the will of God. And when we pray in this way, we know that we will receive what we have asked for in prayer. In fact, as we pray according to God's will, we will soon discover that God shows us how to guarantee that we receive answers to our prayers.

GUARANTEED ANSWERS TO PRAYER

Some people believe that prayer is unnecessary. They say that if God wants something done, He will do it whether we pray or not, and if He doesn't want something done, it will not happen, even if we pray for it.

No one refutes this idea better than C. S. Lewis. He has written about prayer in numerous places. Three of his best essays on prayer are "Work and Prayer" in *God in the Dock*, "The Efficacy of Prayer" in *The World's Last Night*, and what he writes about prayer in his *Letters to Malcom*.[2]

Essentially, the argument of C. S. Lewis is this: Any responsibility in this world which God can pass on to human beings, He does pass on to human beings. God prefers not to do something if a human can do it. God has provided two means by which we can accomplish these God-given tasks: work and prayer. And just as we view work as a way of getting things done in the world, we must view prayer similarly. Prayer is just another God-given way

---

[2] C. S. Lewis, *God in the Dock* (Grand Rapids: Eerdmans, 2015); C. S. Lewis, *The World's Last Night: and Other Essays* (Boston: Mariner, 2002); C. S. Lewis, *Letters to Malcolm: Chiefly on Prayer* (Boston: Mariner, 2002).

for humans to get things done in this world.

Here is what Lewis writes in "Work and Prayer":

> You cannot be sure of a good harvest whatever you do to a field. But you can be sure that if you pull up one weed that one weed will no longer be there. You can be sure that if you drink more than a certain amount of alcohol you will ruin your health or that if you go on for a few centuries more wasting the resources of the planet on wars and luxuries you will shorten the life of the whole human race. The kind of causality we exercise by work is, so to speak, divinely guaranteed, and therefore ruthless. By it we are free to do ourselves as much harm as we please. But the kind which we exercise by prayer is not like that; God has left Himself discretionary power. Had He not done so, prayer would be an activity too dangerous for man and should have the horrible state of things envisaged by Juvenal: "Enormous prayers which Heaven in anger grants."
>
> Prayers are not always—in the crude, factual sense of the word—"granted." This is not because prayer is a weaker kind of causality, but because it is a stronger kind. When it "works" at all it works unlimited by space and time. That is why God has retained a discretionary power of granting or refusing it; except on that condition prayer would destroy us.[3]

This close connection between work and prayer as a means of accomplishing God's will in the world helps give us direction for how to see answers to our prayers, and how to go about accomplishing God's will in this world.

Sometimes I think we confuse work and prayer, and we pray

---

[3] Lewis, *God in the Dock*, 104.

when we should be working, and we work when we should be praying. There have been times in Christian history when the church has focused more on work than prayer, but for the past fifty years or so, the church has focused more on prayer than work.

This brings us back to the subject of prayer meetings, and ties the entire theme together. We might better be able to pray without ceasing and see more answers to our prayers if we let prayer meetings cease.

It is far more popular in many churches to get together and pray about a need in the community than it is to get together and actually do something about a need in the community. Though prayer is a form of work, we must not think that prayer is a substitute for work. Yet this is often what gets implicitly taught in many of our church prayer meetings.

People come together and share prayer requests for the neighbor lady whose husband is in the hospital, for the coworker who lost his job, for the homeless people to find work, and for more people to start showing up for church. These are all valid issues and concerns, but I think that in *addition* to praying for these things and waiting for God to answer, He might want us to answer our own prayers. I think God sometimes makes needs known to us, not so that we can pray about it, but so that we can do something about it.

Praying for needs is important, but one way God wants to answer our prayers is by having us go out to answer our *own* prayers. Sometimes we don't see answers to prayer, not because God doesn't care or doesn't want to answer them, but because God is saying to us, "Answer your own prayer." He lays needs upon our minds so that we can both pray and do something about these needs.

People often say that the church advances on its knees. While prayer is a vital activity of the church, when God presents to us a need we can meet, I don't think He is pleased when we simply present the need right back to Him in prayer. To really see God at work in our lives and in our churches, we sometimes need to get up off our knees in prayer so we can get down on our knees to serve. We need to unfold our reverent hands and humbly put them to work. We need to open our eyes and look around for the needs that God wants us to see and meet.

This is exactly the point of James 2. James 2:14-21 has caused lots of problems in the church over the centuries. With our preoccupation with how to get to heaven when we die, we think that when James says, "Faith alone cannot save him, can it?" James is talking about eternal life and how to get to heaven when we die. Nothing could be further from the truth.

The letter of James is one of the most practical books in the entire New Testament. It is not an evangelistic tract telling people how to get to heaven when they die. Instead, it is a book about how to love and serve one another in the church. It is a practical book about money, favoritism, gossip, and meeting each other's needs. Not once in the entire book is James concerned about trying to determine who has eternal life and who does not.

When we read James 2 with this in mind, we see immediately what James is concerned about. There are brothers and sisters in the church who have need of food and daily clothes. There are others within the church who could meet those needs by providing food and clothes, but instead, they tell these needy brethren, "I have faith that God will provide for you." In modern church lingo, we would say, "I'll pray for you."

James blasts this sort of thinking. He says, "What good is that? Faith isn't going to help in this situation! That's what God put you there for! Don't believe in God to provide for them; you provide for them. Don't ask God to give them food; you give them some food. Don't pray for God to give them clothes; you give them some clothes. "Prayer is good, but when used as a substitute for obedience, it is naught but a blatant hypocrisy, a despicable Pharisaism."[4]

Faith is wonderful. Prayer is good. But a person can genuinely have faith and pray to God without any good works to accompany their faith or their prayer. So the point of James is that the reason God gave us faith is not so that we can sit back and do nothing, waiting on God to act, but so that we can pray with faith and then step out in faith to love and serve others as an answer to our own prayer. While faith can absolutely exist by itself, it does no good by itself. What good is it to pray for someone else, but then do nothing to help the person you pray for? Faith, by itself, is worthless. Prayer alone accomplishes nothing. Prayer, by itself, is not faith, but a lack of faith. For faith to truly be energized, for faith to truly move mountains, for faith to accomplish much, we must join our faith with our actions and seek to meet the needs for which we pray.

Jesus taught the same thing in His Sermon on the Mount when He told His disciples, "Ask, and it will be given to you; seek, and you will find; knock, and the door will be opened to you. For everyone who asks receives, and he who seeks finds, and

---

[4] C. T. Studd, "The Chocolate Soldier." http://www.inthebeginning.com/articles/chocoloate.htm

to him who knocks it will be opened" (Matt 7:7-8). When reading this passage, most people think that Jesus was saying the same thing three different times. They think that in three different ways, Jesus is saying, "Pray; and your prayer will be answered." But there may be a better way of understanding the words of Jesus.

Jesus is not simply telling His disciples to pray, but is giving them instructions on how to see answers to their own prayers. First, Jesus tells them to ask. This is prayer. To "Ask" is taking our requests and needs to God, and presenting them before Him. It is not that He is unaware of our needs, for He knows what we need before we ask Him (Matt 6:8). But just as we talk over the issues of our day with our spouse or friends, so also God wants us to communicate with Him about the issues and needs which are heavy on our hearts and minds. So, we ask Him about these things. This is the first step to prayer.

But after we ask, we don't simply keep asking. We must then begin to "Seek." This is the second step. Seeking is when we look around for how God might answer our prayers. After we ask God for something, the next thing we must do is start looking around with eyes of faith for how God might provide answers to the issues and requests we discussed with Him.

Seeking answers to our prayers leads to the third step in getting our prayers answered: Knocking. After we ask God to help us with our needs, and as we seek for possible ways that God might answer our requests, we must then step out in faith and "knock on the doors" that present themselves. That is, we actively try to find the answers to prayer that God is providing. We might even try to become the answer to our own prayers for someone else.

When we ask, we ask with faith. When we seek, we seek possible answers with eyes of faith. And when we knock, we step out and take risks with faith by pursuing opportunities that were brought to our attention during the seeking phase. Sometimes the first door we knock on is the one that opens, but this is usually not the case. Sometimes we have to knock on ten, fifty, even hundreds of doors. For this reason, the knocking phase is often the most difficult, but it is here that perseverance is vitally important if we are going to see answers to our prayers.

RETHINKING PRAYER MEETINGS

Based on everything we have seen in the previous two chapters, it is high time to rethink our prayer meetings and maybe even say the final "Amen" to them once and for all.

We must recognize the problems of prayer meetings. Most of the bad habits that people use in prayer are learned not from Scripture, but from prayer meetings. Scripture teaches that God is a friend and a Father, there by our side, wanting to have an ongoing conversation with us about what is important to Him and what is important to us. We can talk to Him as we would talk to any other person.

The things we learn in prayer meetings would never occur to someone who had not ever attended a prayer meeting. It is in prayer meetings where we learn that prayer must be said in a certain location, using certain terminology and words, and sitting, standing, or kneeling in a certain posture. It is in prayer meetings that people learn the repetitive use of God's name, strange mystical phrases, or even to revert to the use of 1611 King James English.

It is because of prayer meetings that we feel justified in spreading gossip about others while calling it "a prayer request." It is because of payer meetings that we delay praying for someone when they need it, telling them instead, "I'll mention it at the prayer meeting." It is because of prayer meetings that we often feel it is better to pray about a need than actually do something to meet that need. It is because of prayer meetings that we feel if we pray, we don't have to obey. It is because of prayer meetings that we pray for people to know God rather than actually living a life that reveals Him to others.

Frank Viola has noticed many similar patterns in prayer meetings, and in his book *Finding Organic Church*, he writes this:

> ... Many Christians have picked up a great deal of artificiality in the way they pray and talk about spiritual matters. This is largely due to imitating bad models. To be more pointed: The way that many Christians pray is abysmal.
>
> I would advise against having meetings where everyone offers a prayer request. Why? Two reasons. First, those meetings will no doubt turn out to be highly religious. (In every "prayer-request" meeting I've ever been in, the kinds of things that some Christians ask God to do for them range from the ludicrous to the insane.) Second, those meetings will be the first step down a slippery slope that will eventually become the death knell for your group.
>
> There's a great deal of unlearning and relearning that we Christians need when it comes to communing with the Lord. If the truth be told, most Christians would do well to allow their way of praying to

go into death.⁵

After we recognize the problems of prayer meetings, we can start taking practical steps to help people better understand what prayer is, how to pray, and how to become answers to our own prayers. You may want to cancel all your church prayer meetings, or at least the regularly-scheduled prayer meetings. There is nothing wrong with having a time of corporate prayer on an occasional basis in response to a deep need or issue that is facing the entire congregation. But a regularly scheduled prayer meeting is most often unhealthy for the life of the church, and leads to many of the problems mentioned above. So cancel it.

But this does not mean we cancel prayer. Not at all! With some targeted teaching on prayer and modeling of a healthy prayer life, pastors and church leaders can actually unleash the power of prayer within their congregation. Rather than meet simply to pray, we can show the church how to prayerfully serve the community with eyes to see and ears to hear the needs and issues that people in the neighborhood are dealing with. We can remind the people that as they serve others, they can maintain a prayerful communication with God to listen for what He might be leading His children to say and do. This sort of prayer can set a church on fire!

> Prayer is not a request made to an almighty King who can do anything at any time. It is an act that liberates the origin, goal, and process of the universe from all distortions, poisonings, ravagings,

---

⁵ Frank Viola, *Finding Organic Church* (Colorado Springs: Cook, 2009), 212-213.

misdirectedness, and sheer hatred of being that which frustrates the divine purpose.

When we pray, we are not sending a letter to a celestial White House where it is sorted into piles of others. We are engaged in an act of cocreation.[6]

This is the active prayer life of the church. This is the prayer of faith that moves mountains, feeds the multitudes, cleans up the city, and reaches thousands for Jesus Christ. As a church moves out into the community with prayers of faith and acts of service, the true power of prayer is unleashed within the community of believers, and they begin to see prayer for what it is and how it works.

Let prayer meetings cease, not because prayer is unimportant, but because it is too important to be held hostage in the backroom of a church building. Let us unleash prayer by taking it out of our buildings and into the world.

DISCUSSION QUESTIONS

1. What are some of the things you wish you could change about your prayer life?

2. What do you think about the idea of praying being a conversation between yourself and God? Does this feel right or wrong to you? Why?

---

6 Walter Wink, Engaging the Powers (Grand Rapids: Fortress, 1992), 303.

3. How often do you "pray"? During which times do you feel most as ease, most relaxed, most like you matter to God?

4. Have you ever tried praying to God without all of the reverent postures and spiritual terminology that many Christians and church leaders say are necessary for proper prayer? If not, why not? If so, describe the experience.

5. What is one striking detail about the Lord's Prayer in John 17 that goes against everything we have been taught about prayer?

6. If the Bible shows us that both Jesus and Paul engaged in conversational prayer with God without using flowery language, repetitive phrases, or a special "holy" posture, why do people use such things today?

7. Have you ever become angry at God in prayer? If not, what is holding you back? Do you think God would prefer you to be honest with Him about your emotions than try to hide your feelings from Him (even though He already knows what you think and feel)?

8. Prior to reading this chapter, what did you think was meant by the phrase "pray without ceasing"? Was this possible to accomplish? What do you think of the phrase now? Is it possible to accomplish?

9. What are your feelings about prayer being an ongoing conversation with a loving friend (who is also God) which you can have at any time about anything? Does this excite you

and give you a sense of freedom? Or does it make you nervous? Why?

10. How does abiding in Christ help us learn to pray according to the will of God? Describe the connection between this concept and how you learn to live according to the wills of your spouse, your parent, your child, and your boss (and how they do the same for you).

11. How is prayer more dangerous than work?

12. What is one often-overlooked way that God likes to answer our prayers?

13. Who is the one who will often provide the answer to your prayers? How?

14. If James 2:14-26 is not concerned with where people will spend eternity, what is this passage about?

15. What is James saying in James 2:14-26 about praying for others?

16. According to James 2, how can our faith be truly energized?

17. In Matthew 7:7-8, we find three steps for seeing answers to our prayers. Describe these three steps.

CHAPTER 11

CRUCIFORM PASTORAL LEADERSHIP

Now that we are at the end of this book, you might be wondering why it is titled *Cruciform Pastoral Leadership,* for we haven't defined the word "cruciform" nor has anything been written about pastoral leadership. Let us conclude the book by considering both.

CRUCIFORM

The word *cruciform* simply means "cross shaped, to follow the form of the cross." When I titled this book *Cruciform Pastoral Leadership,* I was thinking of cross-shaped leadership, the type of leadership that has suffering, service, and death at its core and as its goal. True servant-hearted pastors do not follow Jesus into glory and honor, but into crucifixion and death. The cruciform life is the crucified life. It is a life in which we die to self, taking up our cross daily to follow Jesus into the sacrificial service of others (Luke 9:23; Gal 2:20-21).

Quite often, cruciform ministry also leads us to die to the "accepted" form of popular religion and forge new paths of ministry and friendship among those who do not "fit in." I sometimes wonder if Jesus would "fit in" with the church today. Jesus did not fit in with the religious people of His day, and so it is likely He would fail to fit in today either. Jesus reached out to people that everybody—both the religious Pharisees and secular society—considered sinful. And He did it in a way that offended the Pharisees. He certainly didn't join sinners in their sin, but He did join with them in every other way.

> Religious people don't see people; they see causes, behaviors, stereotypes, people "other" than them. ... Jesus' evangelism strategy directly challenged the Pharisees' approach. Instead of "Come and get it!" it was "Go get 'em!" Instead of withdrawing from people in fear of contamination, he ate with them. This was horrifying to the Pharisees. They shrieked their charge against him: "This man welcomes sinners and eats with them" (Luke 15:2; NIV). Instead of insisting that people clean up in order to come to God, Jesus preached that God accepts people as they are ... [Jesus] gave himself away to poor people, sick people, unclean people, the disadvantaged, and disenfranchised from the religion of the privileged.[1]

What would Jesus do today that might elicit similar outrage from religious people? Would He invite prostitutes over for dinner? Become best friends with the child molester? Whatever it was, the religious leaders of today would respond just as the religious leaders in Jesus' day responded: they would be horrified. This is how the self-righteous always react when godly people reach out in loving ways toward those whom society considers sinful. But Jesus reaches out to them, so that He can befriend them and welcome them into the family of God.

---

[1] Reggie McNeal, *The Present Future: Six Tough Questions for the Church* (San Francisco, CA: Josey-Bass, 2003), 28.

If we follow Jesus, then we will follow Him to the cross. Our ministry will become cross-shaped as we crucify ourselves daily and die to the accepted norms of society and religion so that we can reach those who are neglected and overlooked by society and religion, but are accepted and loved by the society of God (i.e., the Kingdom of God). As cruciform leaders, pastors must lead the way.

PASTORAL LEADERSHIP

It is often said that "Leaders lead and followers follow." I have also heard it taught that "You will know you are a leader if you look behind you and see people following." Both quotes reveal the idea that if you are a leader, all you have to do is lead, and people will follow, whereas if no one is following you, this means you are not a leader.

These quotes are true so far as they go, but they miss two of the central truths about leadership, which are also ignored by nearly every leadership book I have read or seminar I have attended. There are two overlooked factors of leadership which few recognize or understand.

The first of these overlooked truths is that while it is true that a leader is not a leader unless they are leading someone, the best leaders actually choose who it is they lead. That is, the best leaders choose their followers. By this, I do not mean that they go out and recruit followers. No, I mean that leaders choose who follows them by where and how they lead. The direction in which a leader is headed helps determines who will follow.

If a leader is headed in a direction of power and prominence, he or she will lead people who also want to gain power and prominence. But if a leader is headed toward sacrificial service and humility, he or she will gain followers who also want to humbly serve others.

Jesus is a good example of this. If Jesus had wanted to, He could have gained quite a following from among the Pharisees and teachers of the Law. He was an expert in the Scriptures, astounding people with His knowledge and insight at the age of twelve. Initially, Jesus had many Scribes and Pharisees coming to Him with questions. He had rich rulers seeking Him out for answers. If He had simply changed a few things about how He answered their questions, Jesus could have been a great and influential religious leader. He didn't have to change or compromise His beliefs; He just had to answer their questions in more ambiguous ways.

Yet in answering their questions the way He did, Jesus challenged the belief structure of the religious leaders, as well as their authority, power, and control over the people. In so doing, Jesus chose whom He would lead: Not the rich, the powerful, and the influential, but the poor, the weak, and the insignificant. In the way Jesus led, He chose to be followed by the uneducated, the outcasts, and the rejects.

It is not that the Pharisees ignored such people. No, the Pharisees wanted the "dregs" of society to repent and return to God as much as anyone else. But the Pharisees required that the sinners, prostitutes, and tax-collectors repent and mend their ways *before* they could be accepted into righteous society. According to the Pharisees, sinners should stop doing what they were doing and return to obedience to the Living God, and *then* they could be in fellowship with one another. The Pharisees taught this, preached this, and modeled this. They were trying to lead the people toward obedience by calling people to follow them.

Jesus also wanted to lead people toward obedience. In this, He did not differ from the Pharisees. Where He differed, however, was in *how* He called people to follow Him toward obedience. Jesus did not call people to reject their path of sin and then come to Him to listen to His preaching and teaching so that they could then be accepted, loved, and forgiven by God. Instead, Jesus went and became friends with the sinners, tax-collectors, and prostitutes and told them that they were *already* accepted, loved, and forgiven by God. In other words, rather than asking people to join Him, He went and joined them. Jesus became one of them.

Though Jesus was an expert in the Law, He did not spend His time sitting in the synagogue waiting for the sinner to show up and repent. He went out to the street corners. He went to dinner with tax collectors. He showed up at places where there were prostitutes, lepers, diseased women, and enemy Gentile soldiers. As a result of this sort of leadership, Jesus only attracted followers who were not on an upward trajectory toward power and prominence, but were instead headed downward, or were already at the bottom of the barrel of society. Due to *where* Jesus led; this influenced *whom* Jesus led.

Of course, as Jesus sought to lead those who were on the downward path, He did this by joining them on the path. This leads to the second overlooked truth about leadership today, which is that every leader is also a follower. Maybe it would be better to say that no one becomes a leader unless they are a follower. The trick, however, is in knowing who to follow. I would argue that the best leaders are the best followers, and wisely chose whom they would follow.

Most leaders today seek to lead the people they think will help them gain more power and prominence in society. Jesus, however, wanted to lead the opposite type of people. He wanted to lead those who would likely be of no help to Him at all, and this desire to lead those who were on the downward path caused Jesus to follow those who were on the downward path. It is like a leadership circle: you must follow those whom you want to lead.

Jesus led people by following them to their homes, their work sites, and sometimes, right into their sin. These were places the Pharisees would not and could not go. As a result, they accused Jesus of leading the wrong people in the wrong way to the wrong places. They had such high hopes for Him, yet He became known as a friend of tax-collectors and sinners; He was called a glutton and a drunkard.

The religious people condemned Jesus and His disciples because He was "doing it all wrong." They shook their heads and said, "If He wants to be respected and well-liked in society, He needs to hang out with different people. He needs to hang out with us!"

Yet Jesus chose whom He would lead by following them into their lives, and because these people were not part of the "approved" group of people chosen by those in power, it cost Him respect and position in society. Ultimately, it cost Jesus His life. But in the process, He became the greatest "leader" the world has ever known.

Leaders today must also make conscious decisions about whom they will lead and whom they will follow. Will it be the rich, the powerful, and the elite? Or will it be the poor, the sick, the outcast, the despised, and the rejected? And once this decision is made, we do not become a leader by calling such people to follow us and listen to our teachings, but instead by following them to their workplaces and leisure activities and listening to them as they tell us about their lives, their fears, and their struggles.

Leadership never works when we only preach at people from afar. Leadership never works when we threaten people to change their ways "or else." True leadership does not consist only of telling people to be godly by following us and our example. It is not wrong to give people an example to follow (as Paul did, 1 Cor 4:16; 11:1), but no one will listen if our only message is that people need to believe like us, dress like us, act like us, and talk like us before they can be accepted by us. True leaders do not have conformity requirements before people are allowed to follow. No, true leaders simply lead, and people learn to change as they follow.

Therefore, we can begin to lead by living among those who need to be led. After all, those we are trying to reach will never be persuaded to follow if they are not within our reach. And the only way to get within reach is to follow them into life. Leadership is not getting people to follow you, but deciding whom you will follow. To put it more bluntly, leadership is not so much about deciding whom you will lead, but about deciding whom you will serve. If you were not a servant to begin with, it is very difficult to become a servant once you are a leader. This present book, along with my book *Put Service Back Into the Church Service*,[2] invites you to return to the position of servant so that you can become the pastor you always wanted to be.

Therefore, when we follow Jesus, we do not become servant

---

[2] Jeremy Myers, *Put Service Back Into the Church Service* (Dallas, OR: Redeeming Press, 2013).

leaders; we just become servants. Leadership that truly follows Jesus looks more like servanthood than anything else. Similarly, when we follow Jesus, we will not become a pastoral leader, but will just become a pastor, a shepherd, who lays down his life for the sheep. This is what cruciform pastoral leadership looks like.

CRUCIFORM PASTORAL LEADERSHIP

This book has been an invitation for pastors to lead the church by following Jesus into death. This book does not provide ways for pastors to better lead the church on the upward path toward prominence and popularity, but instead onto the downward path of service and obscurity. Cruciform pastoral leadership follows Jesus into death and calls others onto the same path.

So death begins at the top with the pastor. The best way for a pastor to lead is to show the church what it looks like to follow Jesus into servanthood. One of the key problems in pastoral "leadership" today is that few people truly understand what leadership looks like, how leaders become leaders, and what leaders are supposed to do with their leadership position. Understanding this will be of immense help to pastors as they seek to lead the church by leaving the church, preach a sermon by being a sermon, show doctrine by living it, and praying by answering their own prayers.

When we pastor in this way, we will truly be pastoring and shepherding the church like Jesus. We will show the church how to follow Jesus into service and sacrifice for the world.

DISCUSSION QUESTIONS

1. How do the best leaders choose their followers?

2. How did Jesus show that He wanted to be a leader of the "dregs" of society?

3. Describe what it looks like when leaders truly follow Jesus.

4. Define the term "Cruciform Pastoral Leadership." How can you apply this in your own life as a leader in the church? What practical steps can you take to lead people like Jesus?

APPENDIX I: PREACHING, TEACHING, AND EVANGELISM

Many people use the words "preaching" and "teaching" interchangeably. Indeed, for the sake of expediency and to avoid redundancy, I have done so myself throughout this book. And then there is "evangelism." It also is a biblical form of communication, but how does it fit with preaching and teaching? This Appendix shows what these three types of communication are, and how we can implement them today. We begin with "Preaching."

PREACHING

When most people think of "preaching," they think of what happens in a typical church on a typical Sunday morning when the pastor speaks for 20-40 minutes about a biblical topic or text to a listening audience.

But this is not how the Bible uses the term "preaching." When the terms for "preaching" are studied within their cultural context, a much different picture emerges. Look at this quote from the *Theological Dictionary of the New Testament:*

Kērussein [to preach] does not mean the delivery of a learned and edifying or hortatory discourse in well-chosen words and a pleasant voice. It is the declaration of an event. Its true sense is "to proclaim."[1]

This dictionary entry goes into great detail showing how our modern understanding of "preaching" is very weak compared to the full-orbed thinking about preaching and proclamation in the days of Jesus.

According to the author of this dictionary entry, the "peaching" of Jesus and the Apostles was the proclamation that the Kingdom of God had arrived. The preacher's task was not educational, seeking to impart an ever-growing knowledge of the Scriptures upon the hearers, but was closer to the task of a herald who travelled throughout the land declaring that changes were coming from the king and explaining what these changes meant for the people of the kingdom.

Since the herald wanted as many people as possible to hear this message, he would usually make it short and pithy so that those who heard could remember it and spread the news. His message was probably only a few words or sentences long, and he repeatedly proclaimed these as he traveled around, while answering questions or responding to objections as he was able.

With the preaching of John the Baptist, for example, the message he often proclaimed was "Repent! For the Kingdom of Heaven is at hand." For Jewish people living under the rule of the Roman Empire, the message of the arrival of the Kingdom of

---

[1] Gerhard Friedrich, "kērussō" in *Theological Dictionary of the New Testament* (Grand Rapids: Eerdmans, 1965), III:683-718.

God was a message that got people's attention and which spread far and fast.

Much of the recorded preaching of Jesus in the Gospel accounts is similar. Like John, Jesus proclaimed that the Kingdom of God was near. Even the parables of Jesus were designed to be short and memorable stories about the kingdom of God and what its imminent arrival meant for the people of God.

So for Jesus and the Apostles, preaching was the declaration or proclamation that the Kingdom of God had arrived, that God's rule and reign was now beginning on earth, as it was in heaven. Jesus "did not expound the Scripture like the rabbis. He did not tell people what they must do. His teaching was a proclamation. He declared what God was doing among them today."[2]

TEACHING

In Scripture, "teaching" is closer to what we would think of as a Sunday sermon, but with a few important caveats. Unlike preaching, teaching is usually performed only to like-minded believers, and usually has room for interaction from those who are present. Friedrich explains teaching by contrasting it with preaching:

> Teaching is usually in the synagogue, whereas proclamation takes place anywhere in the open. Different hearers are present. Teaching is the exposition of Scripture in synagogue worship; it is for the righteous with a view to increasing their knowledge. Preaching is the herald's cry ringing out in the streets and villages in houses. The herald goes to all, to publicans and sinners; he attracts the attention

[2] Ibid, 713.

of those who are without and who do not attend the gatherings of the righteous.[3]

Note the emphasis on the exposition of Scripture as an essential part of teaching.

Jesus as the apostles performed this sort of teaching as well (cf. Luke 4:14-16, 31; 6:6; 13:10), but sadly, there are no written records of what they said during these Bible teaching sessions. Nevertheless, the lack of written records does not mean they did not perform such teaching. To the contrary, since they engaged in this form of teaching every Sabbath, it could be argued that this constituted the *majority* of their teaching time.

So it appears that the modern practice of the "topical sermon" could not be considered as preaching *or* teaching. Teaching is never topical, but is expository, and while "preaching" is topical, it only concerns the topic of the imminent arrival of the Kingdom of God. Modern "topical" sermons about money, marriage, or parenting do not fit within the biblical categories of "preaching" or "teaching." This doesn't mean that such sermons are bad; it just means that the pastors who present such sermons are not preaching or teaching, but are providing something closer to a large-group counseling session or a self-help seminar.

So while preaching is a short, pithy proclamation about the arrival of the Kingdom of God to a group of people (whether believers or unbelievers) so that they are inspired to make a change in their lives, teaching is a longer form of communication to believers only, showing them in a systematic way what the Scrip-

---

[3] Ibid.

tures say and how to apply them to our lives.

DIALOGUE

However, there is one final element to the biblical models of preaching and teaching that set them both apart from the typical sermon in a modern church on Sunday morning. Unlike most modern sermons, the biblical models for preaching and teaching were almost never delivered as a monologue. In nearly all the biblical examples, there is dialogue between the speaker and the audience. The teacher and the learners interact with each other through question-and-answer or objection-and-refutation.

When a herald went through the streets and marketplaces proclaiming a message from the emperor or king, those who heard the proclamation frequently asked questions and often the herald would answer them to the best of his ability. We see this as well when John the Baptist announced the coming Messiah and the Kingdom of God. After making his proclamation, those who heard asked questions about what this meant for them (cf. Luke 3:7-20).

It was similar with Jesus. His declarations about the Kingdom of God generated many questions, such as when the Kingdom would arrive, who would be the King, how the new Kingdom would look, and what could be done to speed the arrival of the Kingdom.

Bible teaching also was not delivered as a monologue. Though teaching has a different audience, a different message, and different content, it was still conversational and interactive in the biblical records. When Jesus taught in the synagogues, it appears that people asked questions and made objections, which Jesus responding to both. This teaching was an interactive discussion of Scripture that probably looked more like a Bible study than our modern-day monologue sermon.

So the modern practice in our churches of a person standing up in front of a group of people who sit passively in padded chairs for thirty minutes listening to a speech about a spiritual topic or passage is not necessarily wrong; it is just not a practice that can be found within Scripture.

Let me emphasize that point. I am not saying that what we do in our churches is wrong or bad. Much of what pastors say from the pulpits might be very good and helpful. But what often is heard from our modern pulpits is not the same as biblical "preaching" or "teaching."

So the modern sermon monologue is not required by Scripture, nor does it seem to have any parallel in Scripture. Since most of the Bible is not prescriptive, but descriptive, we are free to follow the Spirit away from biblical norms, *if* we understand *how* we are doing things differently and (most importantly) *why*.

To properly understand why the modern sermon is so different from what we read about in the Bible, I would need to write an entire volume on the history of preaching. As part of this historical study, we would also see how preaching and teaching were heavily influenced by the surrounding cultural methods of spreading news and educating the populace. Remember, for example, that the methods we read about in the New Testament were not necessarily the "right" way to preach and teach. They instead reflect the ways that news spread throughout the Roman Empire and how followers of various popular teachers and philosophers were educated and trained in the ideas of that teacher.

Sermons transitioned to something more like a monologue as

prominent figures in Roman culture became known for their gifts of oration. Listening to a good speech was not only educational, but also entertaining. So it is no surprise that sermons began to follow this model. This approach to preaching became the most dominant model around the time of St. John Chrysostom (349-407 AD), who became widely known as "Golden Mouth" for his preaching and oratory skills. Of course, when you read the texts of his sermons, you can still see the remnants of a dialogue approach to sermons as he very often responds to questions and comments thrown at him from his listening audience in the middle of his sermon. Nevertheless, the church never really returned to the dialogue method of preaching and teaching.

EVANGELISM

But what about "evangelism"? As I explain in my book, *The Gospel Dictionary*, "evangelism" is an English word that should not exist. It is not actually a translation of any Greek word, but is rather a transliteration of the Greek word *euangelizō*. As you can see, rather than *translate* this Greek word, the Greek letters were simply transliterated, or changed into English letters. If we were to actually translate the word, it means "to declare good news."

This declaration of good news can contain any sort of content at all, whether spiritual or not, and can be directed at any group of people. There are examples in other Greek literature about merchants sending "evangelism" messages to their staff about successful voyages at sea, military commanders sending "evangelism" messages to rulers about successful battles, and mothers sending "evangelism" messages to fathers about the birth of a son. All such messages are "evangelistic" because they have declared good news to someone else.

In Scripture, however, all "evangelistic" messages have a common theme. All "evangelistic" messages in the Bible focus on truths related to the person and work of Jesus Christ. But these truths are not only declared to unbelievers, but to believers as well. Since there are good news truths about Jesus that apply to both believers and unbelievers, this means that both believers and unbelieves can be "evangelized." If you are inviting an unbeliever to believe in Jesus for eternal life, you are declaring an evangelistic message to that person. Similarly, if you are declaring discipleship truths to a believer about how they can better follow Jesus with their lives, this also is an "evangelistic" message.

So when it comes to preaching and teaching, it is not wrong to say that all preaching and teaching is evangelistic, as long as that preaching and teaching focuses on truths related to Jesus Christ (which all preaching and teaching should!). In this way, evangelism encompasses both preaching and teaching, and in fact, is broader than both. One might be able to say that evangelism includes both preaching and teaching, along with numerous other activities as well. What other activities does evangelism include? Well, any conversation you have with anyone else about any truth related to Jesus would be considered evangelism. Similarly, the content of this book is evangelistic, since it contains truths related to the person and work of Jesus Christ. Songs can be evangelistic for the same reason. But conversations, books, and songs are not preaching or teaching.

CONCLUSION

The following chart summarizes what we have learned about preaching, teaching, and evangelism:

	Location	Audience	Message	Goal
Preaching	Anywhere	Believers and Unbelievers	Short, pithy, memorable proclamation	Proclaim what God is doing in the world
Teaching	Gatherings of believers	Believers	A detailed explanation of Scripture	Explain and apply Scripture
Evangelism	Anywhere	Believers and Unbelievers	Declaration of any truth related to Jesus Christ	Call people to believe in Jesus and become His followers

In light of these definitions, we must be careful when reading Scripture to distinguish between preaching, teaching, and evangelism. Doing so will not only help us better understand the Bible, but it will also help us avoid the mistake of confusing either preaching or teaching with what goes on in most of our churches today.

The point of this Appendix, however, is not to condemn what happens in the pulpits of our churches today, but rather to make us think about what we are offering to people from the pulpit, and why. If the leadership of a particular group of Christians believe that large-group counseling sessions on finances or parenting is the best thing to offer, then this is what they should provide. But if the pastor wants to shepherd the flock of God with a good mixture of evangelistic preaching and teaching (as defined in this Appendix), then this is the way to proceed. Each pastor must shepherd the flock under their care to the best of their ability, providing them with the protection and sustenance that the flock needs to live this life like Jesus.

APPENDIX II:
14 REASONS BIBLICAL ILLITERACY IS NOT BAD

Note: This Appendix began as a post on my website at: RedeemingGod.com/15-reasons-biblical-illiteracy-is-not-a-problem-in-the-church/
You can interact with the information below and read the comments of others by visiting the link above.

There are numerous reports circling the internet and Christian magazines that people are becoming more biblically illiterate. Frankly, I am not convinced that the statistics are true, that Christians really are becoming more biblically illiterate. It all depends on how a person defines "biblically illiterate," and I am not convinced that the traditional definitions and tests we use to determine biblical literacy are all that correct. The problem with biblical illiteracy today has more to do with how we define and test for biblical illiteracy than anything else. If we were to define and test biblical illiteracy differently, it might turn out that people are more biblically literate today than ever before!

But I will not seek to perform any such redefinition here. Instead, I simply want to concede the point that people are becoming more and more biblically illiterate. For the sake of argument, I assume this to be the case.

And I do not see it as a bad thing. I do not think it is that big of a deal that people are becoming more biblically illiterate. I actually see it as a good thing. Why? The following Appendix provides fifteen reasons why this is so, but let me state the basic point I am trying to make in this Appendix. The point is this:

> I believe that an increase in biblical illiterate is not a bad thing because it reveals that we Christians are finally giving up the illusion that Bible knowledge is the key to living the Christian life. More and more people are learning they can live biblically without the need to become biblically literate.

I am thankful that studies and reports are showing that people are more and more biblically illiterate, because I think it finally raises the question of whether that should have ever been the goal in the first place, and whether or not biblical literacy ever really even "worked" in helping people live biblically.

In fact, I believe that when it comes to biblical living, everything a person needs to know can be taught to them in 1 minute or less. Don't believe me? Set your stop watch and read the following three paragraphs out loud.

> If there is one thing Jesus reveals over and over, it is that you are loved. More than you can ever possibly know. This means there is nothing you can do to mess up. Nothing. So relax. Enjoy life. Enjoy people.
>
> And as you come to the realization of how loved you are, try to show that same love to other people. You don't need to correct

their sin. You don't need to invite them to church. You don't need to tell them to do anything. Just love them. Love others as you have been loved and as you would want them to love you.

The rest follows from love. Everybody can love, and once you have learned to love, the rest just follows naturally.

Is this everything a person truly needs to know? Of course not! But is it enough to launch people in the right direction toward loving God and loving others, which is the fulfillment of all the commandments in the Bible? Yes! The world would be a better place if Christians simply lived those few ideas above rather than worried about memorizing more Bible verses and scribbling down more sermon notes. Those three paragraphs may not be everything, but they are certainly more than enough. Following the ideas in those three paragraphs will fill a lifetime.

So it is not a problem that people know less about the Bible than they used to. That is not a problem we need to fix. Instead, we need to encourage people to live out whatever it is they already do know.

What is written above is a summary of what follows. The rest of this Appendix provides fourteen reasons why it is not a problem (and might even be a blessing) that biblical literacy is in decline in the church today.

1. THERE IS NO END TO THE QUEST FOR BIBLICAL LITERACY

When we strive to become biblically literate, there is never any end to it. When the goal is biblical literacy, there is never an end to the studies, seminars, and conferences. You never know enough. It becomes an addiction of sorts.

How much Bible knowledge does a person need to have? When the goal is biblical literacy, the answer is always "More than they have now." It's like riches: "How much money do you need?" Only one dollar more. The quest for biblical literacy is a quest with no end, and the problem with the Bible is that it has enough ideas to occupy our minds for eternity, which means that if we keep from stepping out to love and serve others until we feel like we know enough, we will never feel like we know enough.

2. PASTORAL SERMONS HINDER BIBLICAL LITERACY

Believe it or not, sermons are part of the problem. And along with sermons, we can include Greek and Hebrew, theology training, and seminary degrees. All such things hinder the rise of biblical literacy in the church today. It is strange that we use such tools to gain knowledge of the Bible for ourselves so that we can teach it to others, but the end result is that the more we learn, the less other people want to learn.

It is like the fact that there is no such thing as a "Renaissance Man" in modern society. Back during the early stages of the Enlightenment and the Renaissance, there were several men who were able to learn pretty much everything that there was to learn. They were experts in science, math, history, politics, medicine, music, art, and religion. They were able to do this because the overall mass of knowledge was not that large.

But there is no such thing as a "Renaissance Man" today. Why not? Because there is too much for any one person to learn. So instead, people specialize. They focus on one subject and learn as much as they can about it. Even then, nobody can learn all there is to know about one particular topic. Medical doctors, for example, are not experts in all areas of medicine, but specialize in one small subsection of medicine, such as Pediatrics, Podiatry, or Proctology.

Something similar has happened with Bible knowledge and theology. There is too much to learn, and so even among those who try, they specialize is one particular area or topic, such Pauline Letters, Petrine Theology, or Pneumatology. When the average person sees how much there is to learn and the time and effort it takes to learn it, they just decide it is easiest to learn none of it and leave the study and learning to the experts.

So when people hear our sermons sprinkled with Greek, Hebrew, and quotations from theology books, they realize they don't have the time or training to do all this study. Even when they try to gain more knowledge with the limited time and resources they do have, they often get scoffed at or ridiculed by someone with more training and knowledge.

The end result is that while we pastors and Bible scholars have gained Bible knowledge and theological training with the purpose of helping others learn, the way we teach people causes them to throw up their hands and say "Why bother?" A better approach might be to tell people they already know enough. We can also tell them that if questions or issues come up as they love and serve others, they are welcome to study and learn along with us.

3. THERE IS A DIFFERENCE BETWEEN INFORMATION AND UNDERSTANDING

One great problem with the pursuit of biblical literacy is that just because someone knows a lot about the Bible, this is no guarantee that they actually understand what it is they know. In other words, when it comes to biblical *information*, what is needed is not so much biblical knowledge, but biblical understanding.

Everybody has encountered a Christian who is able to quote large sections of Scripture and pass any Bible trivia exam with flying colors, yet who seems to have no grasp about the *meaning* of the Bible verses and trivia facts they quote.

As a child, I attended AWANA and memorized hundreds of Bible verses. But I did not know what most of them meant. My parents also sent me to a Christian school, and in my teen years the school had us memorize large sections of Scripture, such as the Sermon on the Mount, First John, and the book of James. I enjoyed bible memorization, but what I memorized was of no help to me until I began to actually study these parts of the Bible in their historical, cultural, and grammatical contexts to see what they actually taught. It was only then that the information I had memorized became helpful for life.

Therefore, calls for increased biblical literacy and Bible knowledge are not helpful unless there is also an effort to increase an understanding of what the Scriptures actually mean. Of course, that also is a problem, for there are so many various perspectives and views on what the Bible means or how to understand the various sections of the Bible. This is the next point about biblical illiteracy.

4. YOU CAN GET THE BIBLE TO SAY ANYTHING YOU WANT

Related to the issue above that there is so much to learn about Scripture and theology that people just decide to learn none of it is the issue that there is so little agreement about Scripture and theology among those who have put in the time and effort to study.

When people set out to learn the Scriptures, they study, read, memorize, listen, and learn for scores of hours, only to discover that someone who has studied even more came to an exact opposite conclusions about what the Bible means. This is disheartening for most students of Scripture, and so they soon give up trying to study any further.

The more we learn, the more we learn how much more we need to learn. Studying theology is like battling Hydra's heads. You struggle to find the answer to one question, and when you do, it becomes ten more questions. Worse yet, the more we learn, the more we learn how much of what we have already learned is just plain wrong. It's disheartening to learn that no matter how much you learn, you never feel like you are making progress and you can never know if what you learn is correct. Many people just give up trying.

5. THERE IS A LACK OF LOVE AMONG THE LITERATE

One major factor that keeps people from studying the Bible is that the people in our society who know the Bible best seem to be the same ones who live it least. There seems to be little correlation between Bible literacy and Jesus-like love. In fact, for many people, it seems that there is an inverse relationship between love and biblical literacy, so that as Bible knowledge goes up the ability to love others goes down. People typically don't need Bible knowledge to know how to love others. Quite the contrary, an emphasis on Bible knowledge often leads to a lack of love.

As a result, maybe Biblical literacy should no longer be defined as "how much you know about the Bible," but should rather be defined instead by "How much you love like Jesus" or "How well you reveal that God is love."

6. BIBLICAL LITERACY IS CHAMPIONED BY THOSE WHO HAVE SPIRITUAL GIFTS RELATED TO BIBLE KNOWLEDGE

One reason we hear about biblical illiteracy so much is because the people who champion it are the ones who have the spiritual gifts which involve teaching, preaching, edifying, and building up the Body of Christ. One of the great dangers of spiritual gifts is that you think everybody else should be doing your gifts. Spiritual gifts cause you to think that a particular activity is important, and if it is important to you, it should be important to everyone.

But just because you have a particular gift, this does not mean that God wants everyone to have the same gift or desire. Just the opposite, in fact. Yet typically, people emphasize their own gifts when they describe the "best" way to live the Christian life. If you hire a pastor who has the spiritual gifts of mercy or service, his sermons will probably place a heavy emphasis on acts of love in the community and getting out to our friends and neighbors to serve them. He will likely not preach much about the importance of Bible study and biblical literacy.

My wife and I are the perfect example. I am the scholar; she is the server. For years, she felt guilty because she didn't study more, and I felt guilty because I didn't serve more. But we have now come to realize that I study and she serves, and we both need each other. I teach her what I learn and she challenges my views so that we both come to a better understanding. Then she invites me along when she serves. When we go out to love and serve others, I tend to not know what to do, so I follow her lead in helping others.

So one primary reason that so many are concerned about the supposed drop in biblical literacy rates is that the ones sounding the alarm are among those who find great importance in regular Bible study and theological education. They have spiritual gifts of knowledge, pastor, or teacher, and so believe that because God has laid upon them the desire to read, study, and learn the Scriptures, *everybody* needs to do so as well.[1] And when people don't, they feel that these other people are missing out or are not seeking enough spiritual growth. In reality, true spiritual growth in others might have nothing whatsoever to do with an increasing knowledge of Scripture or theology.

7. BIBLICAL LITERACY IS CHAMPIONED BY PROFESSIONAL PASTORS AND TEACHERS

Though this seventh point initially seems identical to the previous point, the key concept here is in the word "professional." By this,

---

[1] See J. D. Myers, *What Are the Spiritual Gifts?* (Dallas, OR: Redeeming Press, 2019) for a discussion of the Spiritual Gifts and how to use them.

I mean that biblical literacy is championed by those who have the "profession" of Pastor or Bible teacher. In other words, biblical literacy is championed by those whose income depends on people coming to them for biblical education and learning.

This does not necessarily mean that they are wrong to encourage people to learn the Bible and study Scripture, but it is important to understand that one of the reasons for their invitations to come and learn is that their paycheck depends on it. You can also see this occur in any other industry. Take the health supplement industry as one example. Those who manufacture and market health supplements must spend lots of time convincing people that they are not as healthy as they could be, so that these people will then buy the health supplements. The first rule to selling any product is to identify the pain point, and where there is no pain point, create one. People didn't know they wanted an iPhone until Apple convinced them that their life was miserable without one.

When I was a pastor, my salary depended on people showing up in church every week. Now that I have left the pastorate and am no longer dependent upon people sitting in the pews and putting money in the plate, I cringe when I go back and read the sermons I preached at that time. Nearly every sermon includes statements about how critically important it is for people to attend church and sit under good Bible teaching (mine, of course). Why did I do this so frequently and who do I never say such things when I preach today? Because my income does not depend on it. Similarly, the ones who decry widespread biblical illiteracy today are also those whose incomes depend on other people paying to become biblically literate.

8. BIBLE KNOWLEDGE IS LIKE AN ADDICTION

The people who are skilled in gaining Bible knowledge are generally those who have addiction-prone personalities. I know, because I am one of them. The behaviors and practices we engage in to study and learn Scripture exhibit many signs of addiction. We Bible addicts need a daily and weekly fix of biblical insights and Bible studies to keep us functioning, and we often eagerly pick up the newest book or binge-listen to the most popular Bible teacher just so that we can keep up-to-speed with whatever is happening in the Bible study world.

There are worse thing to be addicted to, of course. But addictions are never healthy for the relationship of the people in the addiction, and this is true of Bible addicts as well. Bible addicts often have trouble with the relationships in their life, which means that while they may be learning a lot, they are not learning to live it out.

Also, in light of the previous point about pastors selling Bible knowledge for personal income, if Bible students are addicts, this makes pastors and Bible teachers the pushers. This is why you will very often find the most Bible addicts in a church where the pastor places heavy and constant emphasis on attending church, listening to sermons, daily Bible reading, and going to Bible studies. In such churches, however, very little that is truly relational takes place.

Those are strong words, I know, so if you disagree and are in a church that places a strong emphasis on Bible study and Bible reading, try not attending your church for three months, and see what happens. If people call you and tell you that you have been missed, tell them that you are taking a break from church. See what they say. Then see how long it takes for the calls to stop. I personally know dozens of people who have not just done this as an experiment, but have actually stopped attending church for good, and every single one of them reports the same thing: Not only did nobody ever call to see why they were no longer attending or to check up on them to see if they were okay, when they actually encountered someone from the church a few months later in the mall or at the store, that person from the church shunned or ignored the person who had left. This behavior proves that there are few "true" relationships in a church that emphasizes Bible knowledge and Bible literacy. Instead, relationships get sacrificed on the altar of Bible addiction. Maybe someone should start a "Bible Knowledge Anonymous" group.

9. KNOWING THE BIBLE IS NOT EQUIVALENT TO KNOWING GOD

I understand that one reason people encourage others to know the Bible is because they believe that this will help them know God. Since God seeks to have a relationship with every human being, it is important that we invite people to know God and develop this friendship with Him. However, we must be careful to recognize that knowing the Bible does not always help a person know God.

People sometimes say that the Bible is God's love letter to humans, but frankly, when some people read the Bible, all they learn about is a bunch of hate, violence, war, and bloodshed. Furthermore, most people don't understand large sections of the Bible, which makes them think that if God wrote this book to help them love Him more, He must not be very good at relationships. What good is a love letter if the person who wrote it clearly doesn't know the first thing about writing a love letter to you?

While the Bible can teach us about God, it is almost more important that people have a basic understanding of who God is and what He is like before they ever turn to Scripture to learn more about Him. Studying Scripture to learn about God is sort of like the age-old question of the chicken and the egg. You can't really have one without the other.

So rather than tell people to study the Bible and increase their biblical literacy, it might be best for pastors and teachers to first provide new believers and young Christians with a theological framework about God and what they will find in Scripture. This way they won't be as surprised, shocked, or confused when they finally do open the Bible to read what is inside. And we should probably do away with this idea of the Bible being a love letter from God.

One important point to emphasize as well, is that when God wanted to reveal Himself to humanity, He didn't give us a book; He gave us a person. He gave us Jesus. Yes, we learn about Jesus through the Bible, but most Christians already know more than enough about Jesus in order to live like Jesus in their lives. But regardless, it is important to remind people that when they read and study Scripture, anything that does not look or sound like Jesus is not of God, even if the Bible says that a particular event or action is caused by God. Such events reveal more about the human heart than they do about the divine heart.

Let us no longer be people of a book; instead let us be followers of Jesus. And if Jesus invites us to put our Bibles down so you can better follow Him, who are we to disagree?

10. WE DON'T NEED MORE BIBLICAL LITERACY; WE NEED MORE BIBLICAL LOVE

Almost everybody agrees that biblical literacy is just a means to an end. The true goal is not simply to know the Bible better, but is instead to actually live as the Bible instructs. Most people who call for biblical literacy don't actually want biblical literacy; what they want is for people to follow and obey the Bible. This is a good thing.

The problem, however, is that the same studies which report that people are more biblically illiterate than ever usually also report that even those who know a lot about the Bible are not actually living that much more biblically than people who are ignorant of the Bible. In other words, biblical literacy doesn't automatically lead to biblical living.

So if biblical literacy isn't "working" among those who have it, why are they trying to pass their biblical literacy on to others? If it doesn't work, don't export it!

We don't need more knowing; we need more doing. This is why I don't think that biblical illiteracy is a bad thing. Instead, I see it as a clear sign that the Spirit of God is moving the people of God to get their noses out of books so they can get their hands into the world. I see God leading people away from the pews and the Bible studies and out into the real world where we can love, serve, laugh, and cry with the people who are there. And since this is the true goal of biblical literacy anyway, then their supposed "illiteracy" is not really a problem if they are able to achieve the goal while skipping some of the steps along the way.

Should we know the Bible? Yes. But it should never be our goal to know the Bible. The solution to biblical illiteracy is not to bemoan the fact of biblical illiteracy and then seek to make people more biblically literate. We don't need people to know more about the Bible; we need them to show more love in accordance with the Bible.

The objection, of course, is that people cannot live the Bible unless they know the Bible. But again, as we have seen above, you don't really need to know much about the Bible in order to live with love toward others. Most people already know more than enough. Furthermore, since those who devote large amounts of time and energy in Bible study do not actually live more biblical lives than those who devote little time to Bible study, it seems logical that what matters is not how much you know but what you do with what you know.

If I had to choose between a Bible expert who could recite large chunks of Scripture from the Greek and Hebrew, yet who was not very loving toward his neighbor, and someone who barely knew anything about Scripture but who did show love to his neighbor, I would choose the second person every day of the week.

Ideally, it would be nice if everyone was a Bible expert who put into practice what they knew, but nothing in this life is ideal And in my experience, it seems that Christians often prefer to put off loving other people because they fear they won't be able to answer a question properly or won't know how to deal with certain objections or issues that often come up. And so, in a good and godly quest to prepare for the act of loving and serving others, they just attend one seminar after another, one training session after another, one class after another, so that many of them never get around to actually loving the other person. Eventually, the quest for knowledge and for answers becomes an end in itself.

11. BIBLICAL LIVING LEADS TO BIBLICAL LITERACY; NOT THE OTHER WAY AROUND

Most people think that biblical learning leads to biblical living. But it is actually the other way around. Biblical living very often leads to biblical learning. People often think that you have to learn the Bible before you can live it, but many in the church are beginning to see that you actually have to live the Bible before you can learn it.

Yes, I know, this seems impossible. How can someone live something they have not yet learned? Well, they do need to learn a little bit, but everyone already knows the little bit they need to learn. And if they don't know it, they can learn what they need to know in about one minute, as suggested at the beginning of this Appendix. Once people have learned the little bit they need to know, they do not need to learn more until they have learned to live what they already know.

However, as people live out what they already know, issues will come up, questions will arise, and these issues and questions will call people back to Scriptures and into discussion with other Christians for answers and ideas. So living out what is already known leads to the practical and timely learning of other biblical truths as well.

This is called "On the Way" learning, "Just in Time" teaching, or "On Demand" education. This is also the best way to learn something. Humans typically don't learn things very well until and unless they see the need to learn them. And we don't know what we need to learn until the issue or question comes up. When a person goes out to love or serve somebody, they put into practice the little bit they already know, but inevitably, an issue or question comes up that they cannot address. So what does the average person do? They look for an answer or solution. Then they find someone to discuss it with, they look for a book to read, they attend a seminar or conference, or set up an appointment with an expert in that field. Today, they might even search for an answer with "The Oracle of Infinite Wisdom," Google.

This beautiful and timely way of learning is modeled by Jesus. Jesus did not spend three years teaching His disciples in a classroom before sending them out to preach and serve. There was no "Apostles' Seminary" for them to attend before they were ordained for ministry. No, Jesus told His disciples a few things, and then sent them out to put it into practice. When they came back, they debriefed and told Him what they had seen and heard. Jesus answered their questions, addressed their issues, taught them a bit more, and then sent them out again.

This is the proper method of learning the Bible. The emphasis is not on knowing, but on doing, and the knowing follows the doing, rather than the other way around.

People don't need more learning. They just need to go out and live what they already know. Then, if they need more learning, they know what their questions and issues are, and so the answers and solutions mean so much more to them because they can immediately put it into practice and apply it to their lives.

12. MANY OF THE BIBLICALLY "LITERATE" ARE BIBLICALLY ILLITERATE

One of the strange outcomes of calls for biblical literacy is that the people who make the calls are often not very biblically literate themselves. When I listen to the pastors and professors who decry the lack of biblical literacy in the church, I am often amazed to hear what comes out of their own mouths. It makes me wonder about their own level of biblically literacy.

The recent Presidential election in the Unites States is a perfect example. If you were to survey the pastors of the United States about whether God wanted Hillary Clinton or Donald Trump as President, you would likely get a 50-50 split. You would have been able to find seminary trained pastors and Bibles scholars who support one candidate or the other and use the Bible to do so.

During the 2016 election process, I saw a post on Facebook from a popular Northeastern pastor who basically said, "How can any evangelical Christian support the racist, bigoted Donald Trump? Don't you know what the Bible says?" Then he went on to quote some Bible verses which he thought would sway people to vote for Hillary. Not ten minutes later, I saw a Facebook post from a popular Southern pastor who said almost the exact same thing, but this time in condemnation of Hillary Clinton. I don't think he was responding to the first post by the other pastor, but the similarities were shocking. "How can any Christian who truly follows Jesus," he asked, "ever support Hillary Clinton? Don't you know what the Bible says?" And then he went on to quote some Bible verses which he thought would influence people to vote for Trump.

Both of these pastors, I think, would agree that people are more and more biblically illiterate today than ever before. One pastor, of course, would say that Christians who support Trump are biblically illiterate while the other would say that it is the Christians that support Hillary who are the truly illiterate ones.

My view is that both are illiterate. My view is that anyone

who tries to use the Bible to pick a political candidate doesn't really know the first thing about the Bible. But the point is that nobody can really agree on what it means to be "biblically illiterate," and even those who decry the widespread biblical illiteracy of our day would themselves be condemned for being biblically illiterate by somebody else.

13. THE PHRASE "BIBLICALLY ILLITERATE" IS JUST A NICE WAY OF CALLING SOMEONE A HERETIC

This point follows on the previous one. One reason that Christians condemn and accuse others of being biblically illiterate is simply because one group disagrees with how the other one interprets of applies the Scriptures. Christians often resort to name-calling tactics when they don't want to have a substantive argument about the views of someone who disagrees.

In the past, when we disagreed with someone theologically, we called them heretics and burned them at the stake. We do the exact same things today; it just looks a little different. We might still condemn someone as a heretic, but we might also call them a backslider, an apostate, a false teacher, or simply accuse them of being biblically illiterate. Then rather than burn them at the stake, we might try to get them fired from their job or shunned by the community.

These are the tactics many use to avoid understanding the perspective and arguments of an opposing theological position and then doing the hard work of dealing with those arguments logically and reasonably. When someone teaches something that is contrary to your view, rather than take the time to understand their perspective and then deal with it logically and Scripturally, and maybe even correct your own view in the process, it is much easier to just call them "biblically illiterate" and move on.

I get this all the time in my own writing. I occasionally write some challenging things on my blog, and it often seems that when I do, one of the first ten comments is from someone who says, "If you would just read the Bible, you would know how wrong you are. You are clearly ignorant of the Bible." And then they quote a verse or ten which they believe disproves the point of my post. I sometimes comment back saying, "I have read the Bible and am quite aware of those verses you quoted. I just understand them a bit differently than you do."

So the accusation of being "biblically illiterate" is often nothing more than a way to ignore or write off those people with whom you disagree with so that you don't have to consider their arguments or seek to understand their position. And once again, the cry for a return to biblical literacy reveals little more than a complete lack of love.

14. THE BIBLICAL LITERACY TESTS DON'T REALLY TEST BIBLICAL LITERACY

Have you ever taken one of these Biblical literacy tests? I have taken quite a few. They often include questions like "How many people were on Noah's ark? How many plagues were there? How many disciples did Jesus have? Matthew 5–7 is known as what? What is the longest Psalm in the Bible?"

These questions are somewhat of a caricature of the real literacy tests, but they're not too far off. And as you can see, they don't really test biblical literacy at all. What they test is biblical *trivia*.

APPENDIX II: 14 REASONS BIBLICAL ILLITERACY IS NOT BAD

And is that really what it means to be a disciple or follower of Jesus? That we can score 9 out of 10 on a trivia test?

I think what we should be asking people about is not biblical literacy or biblical trivia, but biblical love, or better yet, love literacy. The true sign of a disciple is that we will be known by our love for one another. After all, what good is knowledge of all things if we have not love?

I have some friends who would probably be classified as biblically illiterate. They would likely score a 1 out of 10 on that Bible trivia test, and if you asked them anything about sound theology or central Christian teachings, they probably wouldn't know the first thing about the Trinity, the Incarnation, or Ecclesiology. However, the people I have in mind are some of the most loving and Christ-like people I have ever met in my life. They are more like Jesus than I could ever hope to be.

They are not Bible experts, nor would they ever think of themselves as fully-devoted followers of Jesus Christ. Yet they exhibit more biblical love than almost any biblical expert, scholar, or theologian I have ever known, including myself. Therefore, to condemn them because they are biblically illiterate is to simply show our own ignorance of what God wants for the world.

I have another friend who is literally illiterate. He is in his late 70s and he never learned to read. Furthermore, his wife has a certain illness which prohibits either of them from attending church. Also, because his wife is sensitive to noise, he cannot listen to Christian radio. He has no spiritual input of any kind anywhere in his life. He cannot read the Bible, attend church or listen to sermons on TV or the radio.

I have had numerous conversations with him, and the only thing he knows about the Bible is what he remembers from Sunday school when his mother took him as a child almost 70 years ago. But like my friends above, he is one of the most kindhearted, loving persons I have ever met. Is he biblically illiterate? Of course! He knows next to nothing about the Bible.

But he loves.

And when I talk to him, I see Jesus.

He doesn't need to read the Bible. He doesn't need to gain Bible facts and Bible knowledge. He can't recite the 66 books of the Bible, nor can he list the 10 Commandments, or name the 12 Apostles. If you gave him a biblical literacy test, he wouldn't even be able to read it. The only thing he knows is what he learned about Jesus in kindergarten, and that has been more than enough for him in the 70 years since.

And what is it he knows? Well, I got my "One Minute Guide to Biblical Living" from him. He didn't call it that. The title is mine. But the rest of it is what he told me. All he knows is that Jesus loves him, and that God wants him to love others the way he is loved. And that is what he has been doing for 70 years.

CONCLUSION

If you know anything about me, you know that I am a huge fan of Scripture and theology. I love to study the Bible, and I do so every chance I get. So please do not take anything I have written in this Appendix as a condemnation of Bible study and theological research.

I firmly believe that Bible scholars are absolutely essential to God's plan in human history. Without scholars and theologians, we would not even have the Bible to read, and would therefore have no certain knowledge about God, Jesus, or what we should be doing in the world. So I am thankful for scholars and their scholarship, and I even consider myself among their tribe.

The only point of this Appendix was to encourage the rest of my scholarly friends to stop bemoaning the fact that people don't want to study and learn the Bible any longer. Instead, recognize that Jesus is building His church, and to consider the idea that maybe Jesus is telling people they know enough about the Bible and that they can now go out and start living what they already know. If this is the case, isn't it a good thing that fewer people attend Bible studies today than they did the last decade?

We then can be cheerleaders, ready and able to answer questions and address issues as they come in, waiting in the wings to provide guidance on the foundation of the apostles and the prophets as people go out to build their lives around the cornerstone of Jesus Christ. Let us no longer try to stifle what God is doing in the world by telling people to stop being in the world and come sit in our Bible studies instead. Maybe that is not what they need and not what God wants. Rather than call people in to sit with us in our studies, let us send people out instead, and maybe, if we have the courage, put down our books and go follow them into the world.

ABOUT THE AUTHOR

Jeremy Myers is a popular author, blogger, podcaster, and Bible teacher who lives in Oregon with his wife and three daughters. He primarily writes at RedeemingGod.com, where he seeks to help liberate people from the shackles of religion. His site also provides an online discipleship group where thousands of like-minded people discuss life and theology and encourage each other to follow Jesus into the world.

If you appreciated the content of this book, would you consider recommending it to your friends and leaving a review online? Thanks!

JOIN JEREMY MYERS AND LEARN MORE

Take Bible and theology courses by joining Jeremy at
RedeemingGod.com/join/
Receive updates about free books, discounted books,
and new books by joining Jeremy at
RedeemingGod.com/read-books/

SKELETON CHURCH: A BARE-BONES DEFINITION OF CHURCH (PREFACE TO THE CLOSE YOUR CHURCH FOR GOOD BOOK SERIES)

The church has a skeleton which is identical in all types of churches. Unity and peace can develop in Christianity if we recognize this skeleton as the simple, bare-bones definition of church. But when we focus on the outer trappings—the skin, hair, and eye color, the clothes, the muscle tone, and other outward appearances—division and strife form within the church.

Let us return to the skeleton church and grow in unity once again.

REVIEWS

I worried about buying another book that aimed at reducing things to a simple minimum, but the associations of the author along with the price gave me reason to hope and means to see. I really liked this book. First, because it wasn't identical to what other simple church people are saying. He adds unique elements that are worth reading. Second, the size is small enough to read, think, and pray about without getting lost. –Abel Barba

In *Skeleton Church*, Jeremy Myers makes us rethink church. For Myers, the church isn't a style of worship, a row of pews, or even a building. Instead, the church is the people of God, which provides the basic skeletal structure of the church. The muscles, parts, and flesh of the church are how we carry Jesus' mission into our own neighborhoods in our own unique ways. This eBook will make you see the church differently. –Travis Mamone

This book gets back to the basics of the New Testament church—who we are as Christians and what our perspective should be in the world we live in today. Jeremy cuts away all the institutional layers of a church and gets to the heart of our purpose as Christians in the world we live in and how to affect the people around us with God heart and view in mind. Not a physical church in mind. It was a great book and I have read it twice now. –Vaughn Bender

The Skeleton Church ... Oh. My. Word. Why aren't more people reading this!? It was well-written, explained everything beautifully, and it was one of the best explanations of how God intended for church to be. Not to mention an easy read! The author took it all apart, the church, and showed us how it should be. He made it real. If you are searching to find something or someone to show you what God intended for the church, this is the book you need to read. –Ericka

PUT SERVICE BACK INTO THE CHURCH SERVICE (VOLUME 2 IN THE CLOSE YOUR CHURCH FOR GOOD BOOK SERIES)

Churches around the world are trying to revitalize their church services. There is almost nothing they will not try. Some embark on multi-million dollar building campaigns while others sell their buildings to plant home churches. Some hire celebrity pastors to attract crowds of people, while others hire no clergy so that there can be open sharing in the service.

Yet despite everything churches have tried, few focus much time, money, or energy on the one thing that churches are supposed to be doing: loving and serving others like Jesus.

Put Service Back into the Church Service challenges readers to follow a few simple principles and put a few ideas into practice which will help churches of all types and sizes make serving others the primary emphasis of a church service.

REVIEWS

Jeremy challenges church addicts, those addicted to an unending parade of church buildings, church services, Bible studies, church programs and more to follow Jesus into our communities, communities filled with lonely, hurting people and BE the church, loving the people in our world with the love of Jesus. Do we need another training program, another seminar, another church building, a remodeled church building, more staff, updated music, or does our world need us, the followers of Jesus, to BE the church in the world? The book is well-written, challenging and a book that really can make a difference not only in our churches, but also and especially in our neighborhoods and communities. –Charles Epworth

I just finished *Put Service Back Into Church Service* by Jeremy Myers, and as with his others books I have read on the church, it was very challenging. For those who love Jesus, but are questioning the function of the traditional brick and mortar church, and their role in it, this is a must read. It may be a bit unsettling to the reader who is still entrenched in traditional "church," but it will make you think, and possibly re-evaluate your role in the church. Get this book, and all others on the church by Jeremy. –Ward Kelly

DYING TO RELIGION AND EMPIRE (VOLUME 3 IN THE CLOSE YOUR CHURCH FOR GOOD BOOK SERIES)

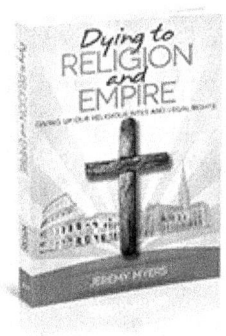

Could Christianity exist without religious rites or legal rights? In *Dying to Religion and Empire*, I not only answer this question with an emphatic "Yes!" but argue that if the church is going to thrive in the coming decades, we must give up our religious rites and legal rights.

Regarding religious rites, I call upon the church to abandon the quasi-magical traditions of water baptism and the Lord's Supper and transform or redeem these practices so that they reflect the symbolic meaning and intent which they had in New Testament times.

Furthermore, the church has become far too dependent upon certain legal rights for our continued existence. Ideas such as the right to life, liberty, and the pursuit of happiness are not conducive to living as the people of God who are called to follow Jesus into servanthood and death. Also, reliance upon the freedom of speech, the freedom of assembly, and other such freedoms as established by the Bill of Rights have made the church a servant of the state rather than a servant of God and the gospel. Such freedoms must be forsaken if we are going to live within the rule and reign of God on earth.

This book not only challenges religious and political liberals but conservatives as well. It is a call to leave behind the comfortable religion we know, and follow Jesus into the uncertain and wild ways of radical discipleship. To rise and live in the reality of God's Kingdom, we must first die to religion and empire.

REVIEWS

Jeremy is one of the freshest, freest authors out there— and you need to hear what he has to say. This book is startling and new in thought and conclusion. Are the "sacraments" inviolate? Why? Do you worship at a secular altar? Conservative? Liberal? Be prepared to open your eyes. Mr. Myers will not let you keep sleeping!

Jeremy Myers is one or the most thought provoking authors that I read, this book has really helped me to look outside the box and start thinking how can I make more sense of my relationship with Christ and how can I show others in a way that impacts them the way that Jesus' disciples impacted their world. Great book, great author. –Brett Hotchkiss

THE DEATH AND RESURRECTION OF THE CHURCH (VOLUME 1 IN THE CLOSE YOUR CHURCH FOR GOOD BOOK SERIES)

In a day when many are looking for ways to revitalize the church, Jeremy Myers argues that the church should die ... so that it can rise again.

This is not only because of the universal principle that death precedes resurrection, but also because the church has adopted certain Satanic values and goals and the only way to break free from our enslavement to these values is to die.

But death will not be the end of the church, just as death was not the end of Jesus. If the church follows Jesus into death, and even to the hellish places on earth, it is only then that the church will rise again to new life and vibrancy in the Kingdom of God.

REVIEWS

I have often thought on the church and how its acceptance of corporate methods and assimilation of cultural media mores taints its mission but Jeremy Myers eloquently captures in words the true crux of the matter—that the church is not a social club for do-gooders but to disseminate the good news to all the nooks and crannies in the world and particularly and primarily those bastions in the reign of evil. That the "gates of Hell" Jesus pronounces indicate that the church is in an offensive, not defensive, posture as gates are defensive structures.

I must confess that in reading I was inclined to be in agreement as many of the same thinkers that Myers riffs upon have influenced me also—Walter Wink, Robert Farrar Capon, Greg Boyd, NT Wright, etc. So as I read, I frequently nodded my head in agreement. –GN Trifanaff

The book is well written, easy to understand, organized and consistent thoughts. It rightfully makes the reader at least think about things as ... is "the way we have always done it" necessarily the Biblical or Christ-like way, or is it in fact very sinful?! I would recommend the book for pastors and church officers; those who have the most moving-and-shaking clout to implement changes, or keep things the same. –Joel M. Wilson

Absolutely phenomenal. Unless we let go of everything Adamic in our nature, we cannot embrace anything Christlike. For the church to die, we the individual temples must dig our graves. It is a must read for all who take issues about the body of Christ seriously. – Mordecai Petersburg

CHURCH IS MORE THAN BODIES, BUCKS, & BRICKS (VOLUME 4 IN THE CLOSE YOUR CHURCH FOR GOOD BOOK SERIES)

Many people define church as a place and time where people gather, a way for ministry money to be given and spent, and a building in which people regularly meet on Sunday mornings.

In this book, author and blogger Jeremy Myers shows that church is more than bodies, bucks, and bricks.

Church is the people of God who follow Jesus into the world, and we can be the church no matter how many people we are with, no matter the size of our church budget, and regardless of whether we have a church building or not.

By abandoning our emphasis on more people, bigger budgets, and newer buildings, we may actually liberate the church to better follow Jesus into the world.

REVIEWS

> This book does more than just identify issues that have been bothering me about church as we know it, but it goes into history and explains how we got here. In this way it is similar to Viola's *Pagan Christianity*, but I found it a much more enjoyable read. Jeremy goes into more detail on the three issues he covers as well as giving a lot of practical advice on how to remedy these situations. –Portent

Since I returned from Africa 20 years ago I have struggled with going to church back in the States. This book helped me not feel guilty and has helped me process this struggle. It is challenging and overflows with practical suggestions. He loves the church despite its imperfections and suggests ways to break the bondage we find ourselves in. –Truealian

Jeremy Meyers always writes a challenging book ... It seems the American church (as a whole) is very comfortable with the way things are ... The challenge is to get out of the brick and mortar buildings and stagnant programs and minister to the needy in person with funds in hand to meet their needs especially to the widows and orphans as we are directed in the scriptures. –GGTexas

WHAT IS PRAYER? HOW TO PRAY TO GOD THE WAY YOU TALK TO A FRIEND

Stop worrying about how to pray, and just start praying!

This book reveals one simple truth: That you already know how to pray!

Once you discover that you know how to pray as revealed in this book, you will also discover that you already know what to pray for and how to see more answers to your prayers.

Read this book and find the freedom and power in your prayer life you have always longed for.

REVIEWS

I LOVE THIS BOOK! J. D. Myers has done such a great job of putting into clear words all the things about prayer that have been developing in my thoughts for years. If you wonder what praying means, if you wonder what praying should be like, or even if you wonder why on earth people should even pray, READ THIS. This is, so far, my favorite Jeremy Myers book. Not too deep, not too theological, not even too serious—though the subject matter is serious and is dealt with seriously. The tone of the writing is perfect, and the advice is genuine and extremely worthwhile. EXCELLENT BOOK. –B. Shuford

The book appears to be too simple but as you progress Jeremy covers many aspects of prayer in a way that is like a breath of fresh air. The book ends up being a natural encouragement to talking to God as a friend. I definitely recommend this book as the reader will definitely benefit from it. Not just intellectually but practically as well. Prayer will change from a chore or obligation to a pleasurable interaction with God. My heart was so filled with joy while reading this book. Jeremy you've reminded me once more that as you walk with Jesus and spend time in His presence, He talks to you and reveals Himself through the Scriptures. –Pete Nellmapius

When you finish this short book, you will know two things: 1) How easy it is to pray, and 2) How dangerous it is to pray! Prayer changes things, I used to hear. I heard in Jeremy's book, prayer changes me. I especially appreciated a page where Jeremy discusses how often we are the answers to our own prayers. I saw a "vision" of someone I am now praying for, and the Lord looking at him and looking at me, as if to say, "Well, I've put you in his life, haven't I?" A beautiful book. –Carol Roberts

WHAT ARE THE SPIRITUAL GIFTS? DISCOVER YOUR SPIRITUAL GIFTS AND HOW TO USE THEM

Let's cut through all the nonsense about spiritual gifts.

Here is a down-to-earth discussion about what the spiritual gifts are, how to discover your spiritual gifts, and how to use them in the real world.

This book answers such questions as:

-Why did God give spiritual gifts?
-What are the spiritual gifts?
-How can I know my spiritual gifts?
-Are some spiritual gifts better than others?
-What are the dangers of the spiritual gifts?
-Have some spiritual gifts ceased?
-What about the spiritual gift of tongues?
-How can I embrace and use my spiritual gifts?

This book also includes a 125-question Spiritual Gift Inventory test.

REVIEWS

J. D. Myers' title *What are the Spiritual Gifts?* is perfect and delivers in identifying spiritual gifts mentioned in the Bible and how to personally discover your gifts to help others. Those who grew up going to church are very familiar with the topic of spiritual gifts. I would encourage those who didn't grow up in the church to read as well if wishing God's help to make a difference in the lives of others through your talents, interests, skills, and abilities.

Those who grew up going to church want to understand more about gifts such as tongues, prophecy, etc. The book does a great job of discussing whether some gifts no longer exist and how we can understand such gifts. –Mike Edwards

Jeremy Myers pulls out all the distractions that keep us from understanding our spiritual gifts given to us from a loving God. –David DeMille

Why do we think spiritual gifts are a mystery? According to Mr. Myers, we shouldn't. In a simple presentation, he offers his view of the Spiritual Gifts, and some of the characteristics for each of them (with strengths and pitfalls). The book also suggests five simple ways of discerning your gift, including a test in the end. While a test can be useful, much more useful are the other ways, like asking yourself what you think other Christians should do more … –The Pilgrimm

WHAT IS FAITH? HOW TO KNOW THAT YOU BELIEVE

You might know what you believe … but do you know *that* you believe?

While many Christians know that they are supposed to believe, they don't know if they actually do believe.

Stop wondering if you have false faith, spurious faith, temporary faith, intellectual faith, or head faith instead of heart faith. All such terms are unhelpful and unbiblical, and cause many Christians to wonder if they have truly believed.

By reading this book, you will not only discover how faith works, but also how to know that you believe.

This book also answers some of your most pressing questions about faith, such as the relationship between faith and works, whether or not God gives the gift of faith, and how it is possible to be certain about your faith. This book also provides explanations for several key Bible passages about faith.

REVIEWS

Once again, Jeremy Myers brings clarity to a topic that many are confused about. Faith is such a difficult subject for some. Do I have enough faith? I have doubts, how does that affect my faith? What is child-like faith? Do I have little faith, small faith or great faith? Many Christians put faith in their faith. Jeremy does a wonderful job of explaining these concepts and more in this book. Having read, and listened to, many of Jeremy's books and podcasts, I can attest to his in-depth knowledge and proficient writing style. Whether you agree with all his points or not, you will come away with more knowledge and understanding after reading this book. This is a book that I would recommend all new Christians read and be used in discipleship classes. –Michael Wilson

I was privileged to receive an advanced copy and am happy to report that the book was enormously helpful. Having a firm foundation of knowing that you are fully loved and accepted by God is essential to spiritual growth, and in our day the greatest impediment to having this firm foundation is wondering, "Have I really believed?" Jeremy helps the reader answer this question. To any Christian who is unsure of your foundation, this book is for you! – K. E. Young

WHAT IS HELL? THE TRUTH ABOUT HELL AND HOW TO AVOID IT

Have you ever wondered if you are going to hell?

Many people are terrified about going to hell when they die. And for good reason. If hell is a fiery torture chamber where lost souls scream in agony for all eternity, everybody should be worried about meeting such a terrible fate.

But is this really what the Bible teaches about hell?

In *What is Hell?*, author J. D. Myers answers your most pressing questions about hell. After summarizing the three common views about hell, this book presents a fourth view. Myers defends this alternative view by showing how the concept of hell evolved over time, and then considers eight terms from Scripture that have traditionally been equated with hell.

As you read, you will learn the truth about hell. You will discover what hell is, where hell is, how you can avoid going to hell, and how you can rescue people who are in hell.

The book includes an Appendix which explains most of the key biblical texts that have traditionally been used to defend the doctrine of hell.

Read this book to be delivered from both the fear and fire of hell.

REVIEWS

My eyes have been opened and my understanding has changed for the better. I believe this book is a must-read for most Christians. The reason for the death of Jesus has also become so much clearer to me from reading this book. It just makes more sense now. This book will be used by me as a reference in the future so I will read it again. –Pete Nellmapius

This may be Jeremy's best book yet! What is more important than defending God's character? Jeremy shows in a scholarly but readable way that the traditional understanding of Hell does not actually exist. The Great News is that you don't have to defend or imagine God tortures people for beliefs while living for a short time on earth. – Mike Edwards - Writing at: What-God-May-Really-Be-Like

I've enjoyed every book of Mr. Myers until this one. But this one I LOVED! The book goes through great lengths in explaining how the Kingdom of Heaven that Jesus came to bring unto our world is opposed to the Kingdom of Hell that rules the Earth. And how Hell has been under siege ever since. –ThePilgrimm

Jeremy Myers does an exceptional job explaining the critical passages of the bible that are typically used to teach that there is a hell waiting for all of us sinners. He always is exceptional in explaining the original text and making it easy to understand. This is a great book if you are trying to understand this topic and I feel you will come away with a much greater understanding. –Jim Maus

NOTHING BUT THE BLOOD OF JESUS: HOW THE SACRIFICE OF JESUS SAVES THE WORLD FROM SIN

Do you have difficulties reconciling God's behavior in the Old Testament with that of Jesus in the New?

Do you find yourself trying to rationalize God's violent demeanor in the Bible to unbelievers or even to yourself?

Does it seem disconcerting that God tells us not to kill others but He then takes part in some of the bloodiest wars and vindictive genocides in history?

The answer to all such questions is found in Jesus on the cross. By focusing your eyes on Jesus Christ and Him crucified, you come to understand that God was never angry at human sinners, and that no blood sacrifice was ever needed to purchase God's love, forgiveness, grace, and mercy.

In *Nothing but the Blood of Jesus*, J. D. Myers shows how the death of Jesus on the cross reveals the truth about the five concepts of sin, law, sacrifice, scapegoating, and bloodshed. After carefully defining each, this book shows how these definitions provide clarity on numerous biblical texts.

REVIEWS

Building on his previous book, "The Atonement of God," the work of René Girard and a solid grounding in the Scriptures, Jeremy Myers shares fresh and challenging insights with us about sin, law, sacrifice, scapegoating and blood. This book reveals to us how truly precious the blood of Jesus is and the way of escaping the cycle of blame, rivalry, scapegoating, sacrifice and violence that has plagued humanity since the time of Cain and Abel. *Nothing but the Blood of Jesus* is an important and timely literary contribution to a world desperately in need of the non-violent message of Jesus. –Wesley Rostoll

My heart was so filled with joy while reading this book. Jeremy you've reminded me once more that as you walk with Jesus and spend time in His presence, He talks to you and reveals Himself through the Scriptures. –Reader

THE ATONEMENT OF GOD: BUILDING YOUR THEOLOGY ON A CRUCIVISION OF GOD

After reading this book, you will never read the Bible the same way again.

By reading this book, you will learn to see God in a whole new light. You will also learn to see yourself in a whole new light, and learn to live life in a whole new way.

The book begins with a short explanation of the various views of the atonement, including an explanation and defense of the "Non-Violent View" of the atonement. This view argues that God did not need or demand the death of Jesus in order to forgive sins. In fact, God has never been angry with us at all, but has always loved and always forgiven.

Following this explanation of the atonement, J. D. Myers takes you on a journey through 10 areas of theology which are radically changed and transformed by the Non-Violent view of the atonement. Read this book, and let your life and theology look more and more like Jesus Christ!

REVIEWS

Outstanding book! Thank you for helping me understand "Crucivision" and the "Non-Violent Atonement." Together, they help it all make sense and fit so well into my personal thinking about God. I am encouraged to be truly free to love and forgive, because God has always loved and forgiven without condition, because Christ exemplified this grace on the Cross, and because the Holy Spirit is in the midst of all life, continuing to show the way through people like you. –Samuel R. Mayer

This book gives another view of the doctrines we have been taught all of our lives. And this actually makes more sense than what we have heard. I myself have had some of these thoughts but couldn't quite make the sense of it all by myself. J.D. Myers helped me answer some questions and settle some confusion for my doctrinal views. This is truly a refreshing read. Jesus really is the demonstration of who God is and God is much easier to understand than being so mean and vindictive in the Old Testament. The tension between the wrath of God and His justice and the love of God are eased when reading this understanding of the atonement. Read with an open mind and enjoy! –Clare N. Bez

THE RE-JUSTIFICATION OF GOD: A STUDY OF ROMANS 9:10-24

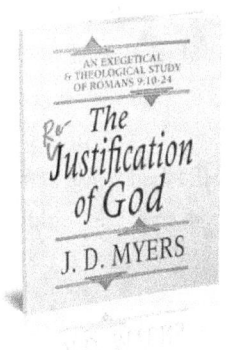

Romans 9 has been a theological battleground for centuries. Scholars from all perspectives have debated whether Paul is teaching corporate or individual election, whether or not God truly hates Esau, and how to understand the hardening of Pharaoh's heart. Both sides have accused the other of misrepresenting God.

In this book, J. D. Myers presents a mediating position. Gleaning from both Calvinistic and Arminian insights into Romans 9, J. D. Myers presents a beautiful portrait of God as described by the pen of the Apostle Paul.

Here is a way to read Romans 9 which allows God to remain sovereign and free, but also allows our theology to avoid the deterministic tendencies which have entrapped certain systems of the past.

Read this book and—maybe for the first time—learn to see God the way Paul saw Him.

REVIEWS

Fantastic read! Jeremy Myers has a gift for seeing things from outside of the box and making it easy to understand for the rest of us. The Re -Justification of God provides a fresh and insightful look into Romans 9:10-24 by interpreting it within the context of chap-

ters 9-11 and then fitting it into the framework of Paul's entire epistle as well. Jeremy manages to provide a solid theological exegesis on a widely misunderstood portion of scripture without it sounding to academic. Most importantly, it provides us with a better view and understanding of who God is. If I had a list of ten books that I thought every Christian should read, this one would be on the list.
–Wesley Rostoll

I loved this book! It made me cry and fall in love with God all over again. Romans is one of my favorite books, but now my eyes have been opened to what Paul was really saying. I knew in my heart that God was the good guy, but J. D. Myers provided the analysis to prove the text. ... I can with great confidence read the difficult chapters of Romans, and my furrowed brow is eased. Thank you, J. D. Myers. I love God, even more and am so grateful that his is so longsuffering in his perfect love! Well done. –Treinhart

WHY YOU HAVE NOT COM-MITTED THE UNFORGIVABLE SIN: FINDING FORGIVENESS FOR THE WORST OF SINS

Are you afraid that you have committed the unforgivable sin?

In this book, you will learn what this sin is and why you have not committed it. After surveying the various views about blasphemy against the Holy Spirit and examining Matthew 12:31-32, you will learn what the sin is and how it is committed.

As a result of reading this book, you will gain freedom from the fear of committing the worst of all sins, and learn how much God loves you!

REVIEWS

This book addressed things I have struggled and felt pandered to for years, and helped to bring wholeness to my heart again. – Natalie Fleming

A great read, on a controversial subject; biblical, historical and contextually treated to give the greatest understanding. May be the best on this subject (and there is very few) ever written. – Tony Vance

You must read this book. Forgiveness is necessary to see your blessings. So if you purchase this book, [you will have] no regrets. – Virtuous Woman

Jeremy Myers covers this most difficult topic thoroughly and with great compassion. –J. Holland

Wonderful explication of the unpardonable sin. God loves you more than you know. May Jesus Christ be with you always. –Robert M Sawin III

Excellent book! Highly recommend for anyone who has anxiety and fear about having committed the unforgivable sin. –William Tom

As someone who is constantly worried that they have disappointed or offended God, this book was, quite literally, a "Godsend." I thought I had committed this sin as I swore against the Holy Spirit in my mind. It only started after reading the verse about it in the Bible. The swear words against Him came into my mind over and over and I couldn't seem to stop no matter how much I prayed. I was convinced I was going to hell and cried constantly. I was extremely worried and depressed. This book has allowed me to breathe again, to have hope again. Thank you, Jeremy. I will read and re-read. I believe this book was definitely God inspired. I only wish I had found it sooner. –Sue

ADVENTURES IN FISHING (FOR MEN)

Adventures in Fishing (for Men) is a satirical look at evangelism and church growth strategies.

Using fictional accounts from his attempts to become a world-famous fisherman, Jeremy Myers shows how many of the evangelism and church growth strategies of today do little to actually reach the world for Jesus Christ.

Adventures in Fishing (for Men) pokes fun at some of the popular evangelistic techniques and strategies endorsed and practiced by many Christians in today's churches. The stories in this book show in humorous detail how little we understand the culture that surrounds us or how to properly reach people with the gospel of Jesus Christ. The story also shows how much time, energy, and money goes into evangelism preparation and training with the end result being that churches rarely accomplish any actual evangelism.

REVIEWS

I found *Adventures in Fishing (For Men)* quite funny! Jeremy Myers does a great job shining the light on some of the more common practices in Evangelism today. His allegory gently points to the foolishness that is found within a system that takes the preaching of the gospel and tries to reduce it to a simplified formula. A formula that takes what should be an organic, Spirit led experience and turns it into a gospel that is nutritionally benign.

If you have ever EE'd someone you may find Myers' book offensive, but if you have come to the place where you realize that Evangelism isn't a matter of a script and checklists, then you might benefit from this light-hearted peek at Evangelism today. –Jennifer L. Davis

Adventures in Fishing (for Men) is good book in understanding evangelism to be more than just being a set of methods or to do list to follow. –Ashok Daniel

CHRISTMAS REDEMPTION: WHY CHRISTIANS SHOULD CELEBRATE A PAGAN HOLIDAY

Christmas Redemption looks at some of the symbolism and traditions of Christmas, including gifts, the Christmas tree, and even Santa Claus and shows how all of these can be celebrated and enjoyed by Christians as a true and accurate reflection of the gospel.

Though Christmas used to be a pagan holiday, it has been redeemed by Jesus.

If you have been told that Christmas is a pagan holiday and is based on the Roman festival of Saturnalia, or if you have been told that putting up a Christmas tree is idolatrous, or if you have been told that Santa Claus is Satanic and teaches children to be greedy, then you must read this book! In it, you will learn that all of these Christmas traditions have been redeemed by Jesus and are good and healthy ways of celebrating the truth of the gospel and the grace of Jesus Christ.

REVIEWS

Too many times we as Christians want to condemn nearly everything around us and in so doing become much like the Pharisees and religious leaders that Jesus encountered. I recommend this book to everyone who has concerns of how and why we celebrate Christmas. I recommend it to those who do not have any qualms in celebrating but may not know the history of Christmas. I recommend this book to everyone, no matter who or where you are, no matter your background or beliefs, no matter whether you are young or old. –David H.

Very informative book dealing with the roots of our modern Christmas traditions. The Biblical teaching on redemption is excellent! Highly recommended. –Tamara

This is a wonderful book full of hope and joy. The book explains where Christmas traditions originated and how they have been changed and been adapted over the years. The hope that the grace that is hidden in the celebrations will turn more hearts to the Lord's call is very evident. Jeremy Myers has given us a lovely gift this Christmas. His insights will lift our hearts and remain with us a long time. –Janet Cardoza

I love how the author uses multiple sources to back up his opinions. He doesn't just use bible verses, he goes back into the history of the topics (pagan rituals, Santa, etc.) as well. Great book! –Jenna G.

JOIN JEREMY MYERS AND LEARN MORE

Take Bible and theology courses by joining Jeremy at RedeemingGod.com/join/

Receive updates about free books, discounted books, and new books by joining Jeremy at RedeemingGod.com/read-books/

www.ingramcontent.com/pod-product-compliance
Lightning Source LLC
Chambersburg PA
CBHW070105120526
44588CB00032B/973